10.50

CHRISTIAN UNIQUENESS
AND CATHOLIC SPIRITUALITY

Catholic Spirituality in Global Perspective

Volume 1
CHRISTIAN UNIQUENESS AND CATHOLIC SPIRITUALITY

Volume 2
CATHOLIC SPIRITUALITY AND THE HISTORY OF RELIGIONS

Christian Uniqueness
and
Catholic Spirituality

Denise Lardner Carmody
and
John Tully Carmody

PAULIST PRESS
New York ♦ Mahwah

Library of Congress Cataloging-in-Publication Data

Carmody, Denise Lardner, 1935–
    Christian uniqueness and Catholic spirituality / Denise Lardner
Carmody and John Tully Carmody.
        p.   cm.—(Catholic spirituality in global perspective; v. 1)
    Includes bibliographical references and index.
    ISBN 0-8091-3197-8
    1. Jesus   Christ—Person   and   offices.   2. Spirituality—Catholic
Church. 3. Catholic Church—Doctrines. I. Carmody, John, 1939–   .
II. Title. III. Series.
BT205.C26   1990
232—dc20   90-42842
                                                               CIP

Published by Paulist Press
997 Macarthur Boulevard
Mahwah, New Jersey 07430

Printed and bound in the
United States of America

Contents

For Harvey Egan

Preface to the Series

Our hope for the volumes that appear in *Catholic Spirituality in Global Perspective* is to place at the service of all Christians interested in the significance of the world religions for their own faith the fruits of recent work on both the world religions and Christian spirituality. In stressing spirituality, rather than theology, we have taken aim at the existential, personal implications of the current encounter between Christians and people of other faiths. In stressing the Catholic dimension of the Christian tradition, we have tried to acknowledge the limitations of our own religious formation.

Although the series is not intended as a work of apologetics, it does spring from a sense that the Christ met in prayer and social service is often undervalued in interreligious dialogue. Inasmuch as we believe this Christ to be the best interpretation of human existence, much of our reflection revolves around how Christians may appropriate the riches of other traditions without threatening the primacy of the Lord loved by the saints and shining from the pages of the New Testament as *the* great event of history. Our intent is certainly not to be fideists, closed to the enrichments and challenges presented by new times, unwilling to reason about the traditional Christian positions. But it is to ease the way of Christian believers to assimilate the experience of non-Christians to their own prayer and service of Christ. The truth we strive to honor is twofold: the holiness manifested outside of institutional Christianity, and the conviction of Christian tradition that Jesus Christ is the definitive savior.

We owe special thanks to Kevin Lynch, C.S.P., and Larry Boadt, C.S.P., of Paulist Press for welcoming this open-ended project.

1

Preface to This Volume

Christian Uniqueness and Catholic Spirituality was stimulated by recent studies proposing a retraction of traditional Christian claims about the uniqueness of Jesus. While trying to acknowledge the valid grounds for such claims, we have found ourselves more concerned to reflect on the difficulty of squaring them with the horizons of orthodox christology, as such christology has formed traditional Catholic spirituality. We take neither "orthodox" nor "traditional" restrictively or oppressively. We are not concerned to sniff out doctrinal deviance or meet a litmus test devised in Rome. But we are concerned to reflect about the Jesus who has been the treasure of traditional Christian faith, because so much of the best prayer and service of the poor has centered on him.

The logic of the sections in this book follows roughly the sequence of essays and topics in *The Myth of Christian Uniqueness,* edited by John Hick and Paul F. Knitter (Orbis, 1987). However, we have dealt with more authors and considerations than occur in that provocative volume, and in the final analysis our book is more an independent essay than a commentary on the work of others. The dialectical, back-and-forth character of the exposition reflects the give and take characteristic of interreligious dialogue, while our final option for an iconic christology reflects the Johannine strain of biblical faith. Finally, in recommending that Christians give the iconic Christ a blank check, we are arguing that the depths of Christian spirituality, as manifested in the prayer of the saints, go beyond the reasons dear to theologians. Such reasons should nourish and stabilize Christian spirituality, but ultimately Christian spirituality is a matter of surrendering oneself to the divine mystery in virtue of the revelation one finds in Christ. It is that ultimate matter that we have tried to bring to bear on interreligious dialogue and the issue of the uniqueness of Christ.

3

Chapter 1

Introduction

Christian Uniqueness

In chapter 6 of John's gospel the following exchange occurs between Jesus and the twelve, his closest disciples: "After this [dispute between Jesus and those who rejected his words about eating his flesh and drinking his blood] many of his disciples drew back and no longer went about with him. Jesus said to the twelve, 'Do you also wish to go away?' Simon Peter answered him, 'Lord, to whom shall we go. You have the words of eternal life; and we have believed, and have come to know, that you are the Holy One of God'" (Jn 6:66–69).

A Christian is a follower of Jesus, the man from Nazareth whom his disciples came to believe was the Christ, the messiah, the holy one anointed by God to inaugurate a new era of human existence. Simon Peter spoke for the majority of Christians when he asked to whom else the disciples should go if they sought the words of eternal life. In believing, and coming to know, that Jesus was the holy one of God, the disciples had found what they had been seeking. Jesus was their master, the one who satisfied their deepest needs and hopes.

Now, the key phrases in this section from John are richly metaphorical. Indeed, throughout John's gospel, metaphor—poetry, symbolism—is the common coin. Thus one is safer in saying that Peter, and those for whom he spoke, found Jesus' words about eternal life, eating his flesh and drinking his blood, the love of the Father, and the like nourishing, consoling, fulfilling than in saying precisely what they understood any of Jesus' capital phrases to denote. Not only do most such phrases have a background of traditional and then-contemporary usage available only to biblical scholars, most are also intrinsically opaque, because they evoke the divine mystery that was the center of Jesus' interest and being.

To say that Peter and the other disciples probably found Jesus uniquely satisfying, a master without peer, one need not torture the Johannine text. What is on the page, and what common sense allows one to make of it, justifies the tentative conclusion that Jesus had no competitors for the allegiance of Peter and the disciples for whom Peter spoke. To understand the depth and range of such an allegiance, the full import of Jesus' conquest of the minds and hearts of Peter and the faithful disciples, one would have to interview Peter and the others at length. It might also be profitable, even necessary, to consider the evolution of Christian allegiance, Christian commitment to Jesus as uniquely fulfilling, throughout later ages. In both cases, however, expanding one's investigation would not remove the metaphorical character of the original Petrine confession. In both cases being a disciple of Jesus would remain an engagement with the divine mystery at the heart of Jesus' interest and being and so something that no words could ever render adequately.

Nearly two thousand years separate us from the Peter whom John's gospel represents as confessing the uniquely satisfying character of Jesus' words. In that long period of time Christian discipleship has gone through many different changes, as has the average Christian's sense of the world. Nowadays people are more aware of the great diversity of human experience than they were in the days of Jesus, Peter, and the author of John's gospel. Nowadays the variety of metaphors human beings have used to confess their ultimate allegiance is more apparent than it was at the origins of Christianity. Followers of the Buddha make it plain that in Asian history millions have found the sutras (sermons) of the Enlightened One vivifying and precious. Followers of Allah, the divinity exposed by Muhammad and the Qur'an, make it plain that they consider the Qur'an words of surpassing value, words for which to live and die. Jews, Confucians, Hindus, Taoists, and adherents of many other religious traditions do not find Jesus uniquely compelling. With or without much knowledge of Jesus, they have gone to someone or something else for the words by which to steer their course. Atheists and agnostics, secularists and unbelievers, have denied that Peter's confession and faith should be normative. For many of them, there can be no normative confession, there is no uniquely holy one on whom to bestow one's comprehensive, religious allegiance.

Caught between the allegiance represented by Peter, which became normative for orthodox, faithful Christians, and the various challenges that other religions and nonbelief represent, many present-day thinkers do not know what to make of the question of Christian uniqueness. After one has admitted that there was only one Jesus of Nazareth, and that the streams of tradition flowing from Jesus are different from the streams of tradition flowing from other magisterial figures, what sort of uniqueness should remain? Does it make sense to say, in the spirit of Peter, that Jesus has the words of eternal life in such wise that it is foolish to seek elsewhere? Or is Peter's confession an anachronism, something that two thousand years of subsequent history and reflection have made impossible?

With now more and now less precision, now more and now less sensitivity to the living religion of the followers of Jesus and the followers of other magisterial figures, scholars recently have been debating the question of Christian uniqueness. More specifically, they have been debating what one should and should not claim for the message and person of Jesus of Nazareth, granted the plurality of apparently viable ultimate allegiances one finds today in either past history or present-day religious activity.[1]

As a result, the "uniqueness" of Jesus has come to focus a great many issues germane to contemporary faith and spirituality. The relations between Christianity and other world religions, the possibility of making absolute claims about historical figures, the significance of attaching salvation to Jesus or any other historical figure, the character of language purporting to capture something transcendent and divine—these and many other issues all can seem to move around the question of the uniqueness of Jesus, like planets around the sun. One need not entertain, let alone settle, them all in order to pray or work from Christian conviction, but one is virtually certain to run into them, if one feels forced to expose one's faith, one's life, to contemporary discussions of Jesus the Christ.

In a later section, and throughout much of this book, we will make clear our own desire to retain the consolation expressed in Peter's confession. For us such a confession, as an epitome of a Christian experience extended and repeated and found anew in most generations, is precious beyond compare. Without denying analogues in other religious traditions, or the need to examine such preciousness in light of today's pluralistic global culture, we want to offer Christian believers help in clarifying their own sense of the unique consolation that the words and person of Jesus ought still to carry.

"Uniqueness," of course, is always in the eye of a given beholder or a given beholding community. At its most interesting, it is an expression of love. Love does many things, but its services to knowledge bear directly on confessions or even judgments of uniqueness. The parent head over heels for the new child finds the child a point of reference so dazzling that all other children pale in comparison. The person head over heels for a romantic beloved sees in that beloved much that escapes outsiders. The language of love is self-referential. It depends upon and points to experiences, perceptions, acts of understanding and appreciation that those outside the circle of love can only imagine. So a first hypothesis for approaching the matter of the uniqueness of Jesus, or any other focus of people's religious (most comprehensive) allegiance, is that love supplies the most precious clues. As the confession of Peter suggests, love both grows from experience of the beloved and in turn makes the beloved uniquely significant, valuable, worthy of full allegiance.

Catholic Christianity

The love of Jesus bound to color impressions of his uniqueness is common to all devout Christians. Still, Roman Catholics, Eastern Orthodox, traditional Protestants, and fundamentalists all tend to differ somewhat in their sense of this love. Their differences are neither hard and fast nor inevitable, yet when one looks at the history of their piety certain distinctions stand out. For example, the intimacy with the human child Jesus that one finds in the Catholic piety of St. Francis of Assisi stands apart from the awe of the Pantocrator, the Ruler of All, that one finds in much Eastern Orthodox piety. Neither sensibility need be foreign to the other. Each tradition could justify the other's piety, and each tradition has housed pieties, forms of religious love, quite different from that of St. Francis or the Orthodox who used striking icons of the Pantocrator. Yet something intriguingly Catholic attaches to the veneration of the child Jesus, while something intriguingly Orthodox attaches to the veneration of the Lord of the Universe.

One could venture similar reflections about Protestant piety and the piety of fundamentalists, and in those cases similar qualifications and limitations would apply. Yet the piety of John Calvin would emerge as different from that of St. Francis, while both would differ from the piety of a present-day fundamentalist such as Jimmy Swaggart or Jerry Falwell. As a result, the Jesus so loved that he was bound to seem unique would be somewhat different in each case. As Jaroslav Pelikan has shown, throughout history different Christian epochs have venerated different portraits of Jesus, adapting the data of the New Testament to their own times and needs.[2]

The piety that we authors know best is Roman Catholic, and no doubt this will color our investigations of the connection between love and sense of uniqueness. Love of Christ is finally so personal a matter that it is hard to generalize about what it is likely to entail. On the other hand, the Jesus portrayed in the New Testament is the common legacy of all Christians, so all Christian piety is bound to be shaped by that Jesus. One of the characteristics of traditional Roman Catholic readings of the New Testament is a certain predilection for the Johannine christology. Without losing enthusiasm for what Matthew, Mark, and Luke have said about Jesus, Roman Catholic theology, sacramental practice, and so piety have had a greater resonance for the interpretation of Jesus that one finds in the gospel of John. Eastern Orthodox Christianity has shared this tendency, and both have therefore developed spiritualities, loves of Jesus, that made his humanity the great metaphor for the divine life, light, and love. Somewhat in contrast, Protestant Christianity has favored the interpretation of Jesus and the gospel laid out in the Pauline literature, though of course it has not neglected either the synoptic gospels or the gospel of John. Fundamentalist Christians, the majority of whom align themselves with Protestantism, tend, interestingly, to stress the Johannine portrait of Jesus (or at least Johannine sayings about Jesus), because the Johannine materials offer the clearest testimonies to the divinity of Jesus. However, fundamentalist Christians almost by definition downplay the metaphoric character of such Johannine testimonies, because metaphor destroys the univocal, literal mentality that fundamentalism requires. Relatedly, fundamentalist Christians are uneasy with a sacramental piety, a love of Jesus married to encounters with him through bread and wine, water and oil.

To say the least, all of this is a rough and ready sketch of some differences among the different traditions' approaches to Jesus. Our aim is only to suggest why it is useful to underscore the Catholic tradition from which we, and the primary audience we have targeted, come.

Ecumenical Christians, sophisticated enough to realize that the traditions need one another to supplement their respective deficiencies, should not find the Catholicity we present problematic. It has been significant in the piety of the great Protestant and Orthodox spiritual teachers, just as much of the marrow of the Protestant and Orthodox spiritual geniuses has been significant in the piety of the great Roman Catholic spiritual teachers. For example, St. Thomas Aquinas shared many of the convictions about the primacy of conscience and the need for religious freedom that animated the classical Protestant reformers. The Benedictine spiritual tradition has been so liturgical as to make many of its instincts about the paschal Christ, crucified and risen, similar to those of Eastern Orthodoxy, where monasticism also was greatly shaped by the liturgy.

In considering Catholic loves of Christ and so experiential senses of Christ's uniqueness, we have to admit that a full range of approaches has flourished. St. Ignatius Loyola and the Jesuits have been distinguishable from St. John of the Cross, St. Teresa of Avila, and the Carmelites. On the other hand, both have been mystical traditions, as have all the major Catholic spiritualities. All, in other words, have made living contact with the Christ alive in the New Testament, alive in the liturgy, and alive in believers' hearts crucial. Such living contact brought the believer into the mysteriousness of Jesus the Christ. No one who prayed faithfully and received intimations of Christ's life could understand fully the implications of being related to him. No one who sought the Father of Christ or the Spirit of Christ and came away satisfied in spirit could say precisely what had happened. Living contact with the Christian divinity brought people into a darkness that challenged their natural expectation to understand and gain control. So regularly as to seem virtually necessary, people intimately involved with Jesus, people of prayer and devotion and service, felt their boats slip their moorings and drift out onto uncharted waters. A living Christ, an existential God, was a sovereign master, a creative Lord, in such wise that any faithful disciple was thrown into a power and beauty ever ancient and ever new, always challenging and often consoling, but never subject to human control.

Any warmth that disciples felt for the human Jesus folded into this mysteriousness. One whose heart went out to the child Jesus in the manger, or the suffering Jesus on the cross, was carried farther from shore. The movement tended to be away from preconceptions and securities, away from what the crowd assumed or the common people expected. Indeed, the spiritual movement consequent on intimacy with Jesus was away from what the person himself or herself initially expected. Why? Because intimacy with Christ made it clear that the God at his center held all the priority, and that this priority was moral as well as ontological—in goodness as well as in being. In a word, intimacy with Christ made it clear that one was a sinner, a person unable to measure up to Christ's standards and call. Again and again, one had been stupid, unfaithful, cold, distant, afraid to accept the overtures of the divine love. So one was heartened by the evangelical talk about the need to forgive seventy times seven, and one's love of Jesus carried more and more a note of gratitude. The very possibility of reaching out toward Jesus, of wanting friendship and love, depended on Jesus' having first reached out to oneself. Only the pure goodness of the divine, as revealed and warranted by the behavior of Jesus, allowed those who matured in prayer to keep on hoping that their searches, their desires to love, might be accepted. The uniqueness of Jesus was the warrant Jesus gave for thinking, hoping, trusting that this nearly incredible prospect of acceptance might be possible, indeed likely. The wonder of Jesus was the goodness of the divinity he revealed, a goodness so beyond human calculation that it made the world turn over and creation reconfigure itself. If one grew intimate with Jesus, human sinfulness assumed staggering proportions. All of the darkness and obtuseness that kept human beings from doing what was in their truly best interests, from doing what their very constitution as beings born of the divine love demanded, loomed as a mystery of iniquity, a fault so original that it sent cracks rippling through all human institutions: the family, the state, the corporation, even the church. So Catholic Christianity came to regard Jesus the Christ as the great sacrament of God's forgiveness. The love manifested in the death and resurrection of Christ was the love that made him uniquely able to save humankind from its deadly alienations.

Spirituality

In speaking about Catholic approaches to Jesus, we have been discussing spirituality. To be sure, we have also implied historical and theological matters, but our focus has stayed on Catholic spirituality. By "spirituality" we mean the lived, personal dimensions of faith,

where the call to prayer and service is existential: something whole and
pressing. The majority of human beings, throughout history, have employed their religious traditions, indeed their entire cultural traditions,
to spiritual ends. Their use of Hindu or Buddhist traditions, African or
native American cultural complexes, was to gain meaning and order.
They were not detached theologians or historians. They were not
scholars or political leaders. They were simply ordinary people seeking
a path through the wilderness of human experience. What they needed
was light and warmth, food for their minds and food for their hearts.
When they found light and warmth, they called their traditions good.
When they wandered in the dark and the cold, they wondered whether
their traditions were still viable.

So spirituality has been virtually the same as most human beings'
searches for wisdom and ecstasy. It has involved all sorts of people, from
both sexes, all races, and all socioeconomic classes, in the pursuit of
sense, meaning, fulfillment. The great trigger to spiritual searching,
historically, has been dissatisfaction and suffering. Tasting ashes or
wormwood, people have resolved to find genuine nourishment for their
souls. Encountering evil or harsh fate, people have left their old sense
of reality behind and set out to find something deeper, something so
profound that it might make death and injustice penultimate. To be
human was to be realistic about one's world. To be wise was to know, in
ways that pacified one's soul and made one a guide and comfort to
others, what was possible, in both human affairs and intercourse with
more than human powers.

Described in this way, spirituality is exciting. It calls to mind Socrates making the love of wisdom the great project of his life. It calls to
mind the Buddha, vowing that he would not move until he had solved
the problem of suffering. And it calls to mind Jesus, convinced that the
sovereign God of Israel was a loving parent passionately desiring to
right human disorders and create a new eon.

These three figures are giants, standing on any fair list of humanity's benefactors as primary sources of light and warmth. Each was
passionately involved in the quest or mission that dominated his life.
Each felt that time apart from this quest was at best a respite, more
frequently a loss. In their passion, each of these three figures revealed
that wisdom, a full humanity realistic about what human beings might
expect, was a function of love. Socrates loved wisdom, even though he
realized it mainly amounted to knowing that he did not know a fraction

of what he wanted to know, a fraction of what his humanity seemed to require. The Buddha loved release from suffering, the healed humanity that could emerge when people freed themselves of desire and let the world come to them, in freedom, as it would. Jesus loved the divine mystery he called his Father, trusting that he could do nothing more useful, more pleasing to the Father or beneficial to his fellow human beings, than surrender himself completely to the Father's will.

It only remains to be noted that the foremost followers of these and the other great benefactors of humankind have imitated them in making their path, their existential searching, a matter of great passion. The saints that the great spiritual traditions honor as the best disciples of the original master or the best servants of the master's God have fallen in love with the prospect the master's way held out. With time, they have realized that the way mediated the divine mystery from the beginning. It was not a way that delivered results only at the end, only at death. When one followed, got in tune with, the spiritual movements exemplified by Socrates, or the Buddha, or Jesus, one met the mystery that had seized their minds, hearts, souls, and strengths. Reading the Platonic dialogues, or the Buddhist sutras, or the gospels with a passionate spirit, the spirit of a seeker and lover, one would be moved regularly to exit the quotidian, average reality one usually inhabited and meet the idea of the Good, or the prospect of nirvana, or the Father of Christ. It was difficult to describe such a spiritual movement, and even more difficult to say why it was so satisfying. Indeed, the longer one persevered in it, the more paradoxical it became, for it tended to bring one difficulties, sufferings, a loss of orientation. None of these, however, overbalanced the necessities and satisfactions it involved. Even when one's spirit seemed lost in a dark night, abandoned to a cloud of unknowing, one's spirit could find nothing better to do or want than to abide with the divine mystery once revealed to it.

We could multiply descriptions of spirituality endlessly, because the tie of spirituality to the divine mystery makes the implications of spirituality inexhaustible. Inasmuch as that mystery is the beginning and the beyond of human consciousness, as Eric Voegelin has noted, it actually structures, indeed even constitutes, human consciousness— the awareness that separates us from lower animals.[3] Suffice it for present purposes, however, to link this description of spirituality with the question of the uniqueness of Jesus. Translating Peter's remarks about Jesus being the only one to whom the disciples wanted to go, with whom the disciples wanted to abide, we can say a given religious tradition's sense of the uniqueness of the one to whom it owes its life is a function of spiritual encounters with, or occasioned by, that beneficial person. One could say that Peter might have found words of everlasting life in the torah that was his birthright as a Jew. Quite right, but in fact it was his dealings with Jesus that became the pivot of his life, the generator and sustainer of his passionate spirituality. Whether or not he might have found his way by following another rabbi is therefore a moot question. One of the many aspects of the mysteriousness of human existence is the effects of apparently accidental but actually providential encounters. To the secular mind, which was little represented in Peter's cultural milieu, Peter's meeting with Jesus could have seemed a chance occurrence. To the religious mind, convinced of the priority of the mystery at the beginning and the beyond of human existence, the height and the depth, nothing is accidental. Everything is part of a comprehensive pattern set in the mind of God. Why this conviction about providence does not mean that evolution and history are predetermined involves considerable hard thinking about the existence of God and the character of the divine intelligence. It is enough for present purposes to note that God does not exist in time, so there is no before and after in the divine knowing, and to underscore the practical implications of a providential view of the specific ways people have found their words of everlasting life. Few of them have shopped outside their own natal culture. Most human beings have considered their spiritual masters unique because their spiritual masters have seemed to carry the same necessity and surprise as the rest of their existence as European Jews, or Latin American Catholics, or Tibetan Buddhists, or North American secularists strangely haunted by Socrates.

When taken as a function of spirituality, then, uniqueness seems virtually inevitable. The choice of one's master, and the experiences of satisfaction, love, and immersion in divine mystery associated with that choice, are inseparable from the road one actually travels. Antecedently, that road can seem a matter of happenstance, of turning left rather than right at the fork in the yellow wood. At its end, or even in its middle, however, the road, one's life, acquires a certain necessity. As a result, the treasure one set one's heart upon, the master one came to revere, acquires a certain necessity. In time, one's life is inseparable from the discipleship one chose, and so one's master carries the same uniqueness as one's own irreplaceable existence. No one else has ever been John Smith or Mary Jones with exactly the physical attributes and lifetime of experiences making up one's self. No one else has been discipled to Jesus or the Buddha precisely as oneself has. So no one else could have had the words of everlasting life that saw one through and turned one's heart aglow.

This Book

Our goal in this book is an examination of the uniqueness of Jesus, including the special value that Christians have found in intimacy with Jesus. We make this examination in light of recent discussions of the uniqueness of Jesus that have cast doubt on traditional Christian claims. For the participants in such discussions, the long-standing theses about the divinity of Jesus and his necessity for any person's salvation require a sober rethinking. Spurred by present-day awareness of the great diversity of paths that human beings have taken toward meaning and fulfillment, many present-day scholars of religion find any portentous claims for the uniqueness of Jesus inadmissible, perhaps even dangerous.

We examine the contours of this position in the next chapter, explaining why the opponents of strong claims for the uniqueness of Christ think that historical consciousness, the transcendence of God, social justice, and other factors much on the minds of contemporary scholars of religion render the pronouncements of classical church councils such as Chalcedon passé. We also indicate the irrelevance of much of this discussion to the spiritual convictions of the passionate follower of Jesus.

Using such recent discussion as a springboard, we turn to the valid aspects of recent efforts to delimit the Christian claims for the uniqueness of Jesus. From Christian grounds themselves, as well as from studies in the history of religion, we consider the ways in which human beings are more alike than diverse, the ways in which its humanity has limited Christianity, the beneficial aspects of considering human religiosity a pluralistic affair, and so forth. Our point is that orthodox Christian theology, and praiseworthy convictions of much Christian spirituality, raise pressure to keep Christians from overlooking the implications of the full humanity of Christ, as well as the implications of God's desire to save all human beings and share divine life with them.

Chapter 4 takes up the reverse side of the coin. There are strong reasons for retaining many traditional Christian instincts about the uniqueness of Jesus the Christ; in this chapter we enumerate many of them. Here it becomes clear that those proposing the abandonment of traditional Christian claims about the uniqueness of Christ seldom speak from within the precincts of Christian devotion or spirituality. The love of the committed disciple carries no weight in their calculations, much to their loss. Without such love, as noted, one cannot speak about God, cannot expose a full knowledge of God, as the most exemplary Christians have. So the topics we take up in pursuing the rightful Christian claims about the uniqueness of Christ are illumined by our convictions about spirituality. As well, they are powered by the conviction that the first obligation of Christian theologians and spiritual writers is to render Christian experience on its own terms. Only after one has faithfully exposed what devout Christians have tended to think about Jesus can one move to the translations necessary to make sense of such thoughts apart from specifically Christian faith and love. People of other faiths naturally can request similar treatment, arguing that when their convictions are not rendered from the inside, what they love and find unique is not made clear. This legitimate request sets the stage for questions about interreligious dialogue. Even though interreligious dialogue is not our direct concern, arguing for the proper uniqueness of Christ inevitably involves us with the ground-rules for discussions between the adherents of different masters, traditions, and spiritual ways.

Our final chapter brings what we have discovered about the limitations of claims for the uniqueness of Christ, and the ways in which certain claims remain valid, to bear on Catholic spirituality. While we are interested in the speculative side of Christian uniqueness, our greater interest is interpreting what the present debate implies for the actual living of Christian faith. If we are successful, the reader should find answers, or at least pointers to answers, to several questions that now float in the air of American culture, often troubling Christian faith, prayer, and service of the poor. For example, how can one defend one's piety against the charge that history, the temporality of human existence, relativizes all claims and commitments? How can one accept the maleness of Jesus without condemning female Christians to second-class status? What may a devout follower of Jesus think about the achievements of a Buddha, or a Muhammad, or a Lao Tzu?

Our three main chapters (3, 4, and 5) amount to a contemporary appreciation of Jesus—a contemporary christology. The distinctive note of this christology, however, is its bent toward spirituality. We are not interested in historical or doctrinal matters for their own sake, but only inasmuch as they bear on how those wanting to meet and follow Jesus ought to think. This concern with spirituality is not an effort to depreciate the history of Christian faith, or speculative christology, or comparative religious studies, or any other intellectual inquiry, academic or creative. It is simply an effort to retain a clear focus on what the so many implications spinning off from the current discussions about the uniqueness of Christ mean for Christian discipleship— Christian intercourse with Christ and effort to serve him.

If asked for a theological thesis justifying our interest, we would bring forward the notion that one advances in uniqueness in the measure that one draws close to God. This notion can have an apologetic cast, defending the proposition that abandonment to the will of God does not mean the loss, but rather the perfecting, of human freedom (and so of human individuality). But we are more interested in its theological and spiritual core. Theologically, the best explanations of creation, in our view, make finite existence a share in divine being. Without confusing creature and creator, finite and infinite, the best exponents of the Christian doctrine of creation make it plain that everything positive in the world and human beings comes from God. The puzzle, it follows, is not how there can be a God but how there can be limited beings, creatures. For faith, God is self-sufficient. Creatures are not. Only God gives creatures their reason to be. It further follows that free creatures are most realistic when they appreciate their complete dependence upon God. With such appreciation, they know what limited beings can learn of their place in the overall scheme of things and most clearly express their divine source as that source intended them to do.

All of this is a somewhat metaphysical way of talking about the foundations of the common human experience that ecstasy brings one alive, makes one feel most oneself. Ecstasy is stepping outside of ordinary consciousness and sensing the totality, the strictly divine mystery, in which one is immersed. The saints, for whom ecstasy was habitual, realized that only by appreciating this mystery and basing their calculations on it would any human beings be truly realistic. The divine mystery is the most fundamental fact in our world, even though the majority of human beings seem to ignore it. In a word, then, the movements that take people into the divine mystery are the richest source of their self-realization and so of their proper uniqueness. For Christians all this is colored by Christ, whom they take to be the unique revelation of God to whom they go for the words of everlasting life. So losing one's Christian life and finding it become functions of fidelity to Christ—a good note on which to end our Introduction and pass on to recent discussion of what one may legitimately claim for such a fidelity.

NOTES

1. See, for example, Paul F. Knitter, NO OTHER NAME? (Maryknoll, N.Y.: Orbis, 1985); John Hick and Paul F. Knitter, eds., THE MYTH OF CHRISTIAN UNIQUENESS (Maryknoll, N.Y.: Orbis, 1987); Leonard Swidler, ed., TOWARD A UNIVERSAL THEOLOGY OF RELIGION (Maryknoll, N.Y.: Orbis, 1987).

2. See Jaroslav Pelikan, JESUS THROUGH THE CENTURIES (New Haven: Yale University Press, 1985).

3. See Eric Voegelin, THE BEGINNING AND THE BEYOND (Chico, Cal.: Scholars Press, 1984).

Chapter 2

Recent Challenges to
the Uniqueness of Christ

Historical Consciousness and Relativity

The theologian Gordon Kaufman has written: "If we understand historicity in the sense I am urging here, Christian faith (like every other faith) will be seen as one perspective, one worldview, which has developed in and through a long history alongside other traditions, many of which are vying for the attention and loyalty of us all today. When one applies the concept 'worldview' to one's own tradition in this way, one simultaneously distinguishes it from and relates it to other worldviews. This involves a certain distancing of oneself from one's tradition, taking a step back from simple, unmediated commitment to it. We now see the great theologians of Christian history, for example, not simply as setting out the truth that is ultimately salvific for all humanity (as they have often been understood in the past), but rather as essentially engaged in discerning and articulating one particular perspective on life among many others."[1]

The perspective Kaufman takes in this quotation is not that of committed Christian faith. He has moved outside the circle of Christian commitment, to a position from which he can survey Christianity alongside other world religions. For the sake of having a name, we may call this position the standpoint of "religious studies," the discipline that has established itself in many universities. Departments of religious studies attempt to deal with religion with the detachment, the objectivity, of the historian studying the French Revolution or the sociologist studying the marital patterns of nineteenth century Muscovites. From such a detached point of view, it makes sense to arrange Christianity alongside Hinduism and Buddhism, Judaism and Islam. Equally, it makes sense to compare claims made for Jesus with claims made for Confucius, or Krishna, or Buddha, or Muhammad.

Several questions arise, however, and elaborating them may help us begin to clarify what is involved in appreciating the uniqueness that a contemporary Christian spirituality may claim to find in Jesus Christ. First, there are the existential implications of assuming the outside, detached stance we have associated with religious studies. Such a stance is a scholarly convenience, useful when one wishes to survey a variety of competing claims. On the other hand, it leaves hanging the question of what one is to make of such detachment, how such detachment squares with the existential task, incumbent on all human beings, of finding one's way in the world. The religious traditions that scholarship in religious studies surveys all make existential claims. Each says that one can only fully appreciate the truth it proposes by consorting with a commitment to the discipline and assumptions it makes. For example, Buddhists say that one has to practice the precepts of the Buddha, through meditation and observing Buddhist ethical imperatives, if one is to grasp the full significance of "enlightenment," "suffering," "detachment," and the other key Buddhist notions. Muslims say that one cannot estimate the significance of Muhammad rightly unless one has submitted oneself to Allah and the Qur'an. And Christians take an equally existential position. For Christians only those who do the truth come to the light, and the truth Christians have in mind is inseparable from the revelation of Christ that solicits their faith.

Thus a dialogue, if not a confrontation, lurks in the believer's meeting with a position such as Kaufman's. Useful as Kaufman's understanding of historicity may be, what does it imply for personal faith, the central act by which a person makes the commitment necessary to follow a definite path through time and experience? More pointedly, is the stance of the religious studies scholar itself a pathway, an alternate religion? Such a question may seem foolish, until one realizes that scholarly detachment itself implies a worldview. At the least, it says that certain kinds of truth only emerge when one prescinds from existential commitments to particular pathways through life. At its strongest, it says that the most basic commitment of the scholar, and perhaps of any properly sophisticated person, ought to be to such detachment. Correlatively, the strong version of the philosophy or operational thesis of the religious studies scholar implies that a proper awareness of historicity relativizes all absolute or imperative claims. The scholar ought to be skeptical of any claims that a Buddha, Muhammad, or Jesus has discovered or been given insights valid for all people, insights mediating salvation to anyone willing to embrace them. One cannot allow that such claims, with their links to a reality (nirvana, Allah, the Father of Jesus) supposedly transcending history, can emerge validly from the experience of historical figures.

What happens when one asks the historicist for a positive elaboration of the commitments entailed in historicism itself? Suppose one is so vulgar as to inquire what historicism offers people to live by; what reply comes back? Usually there is no reply. Usually the question is ruled inadmissible. Existential matters, questions of ultimate commitment, questions of what to live by are considered personal in the sense of one's own business. They are not something that should factor into the public, detached discussion of the religious options that people have exercised throughout history. Granted, most such people have thought (because their religions told them to think) that one had to choose for or against God. Not to choose for Jesus or Allah was to choose against Jesus or Allah—to remain in unbelief. "Unbelief" was an existential state, a cast of soul. And unbelief had momentous implications. Even when one rejects the political conclusions that Muslims and Christians sometimes drew, saying that they should never have made unbelievers second class citizens, let alone murdered them as infidels, something acute remains. The stance one takes toward claims about ultimate reality, about God and God's claims, shapes one's soul. There is no such thing as scholarly detachment when it comes to the existential personality. Either one in fact is living with scholarly detachment as one's ultimate truth, or one is living in confusion, not matching the claims one makes for scholarly detachment with the way one approaches death, Jesus, the needs of the poor, and the other personal challenges that reveal one's actual values. Such confusion may or may not be hypocritical, but it does not exempt one from the task of matching one's knowing (or claiming) with one's doing, one's living. Nothing can exempt any of us from this task.

We all have a religion, in the sense of a treasure we've set our heart upon. If our treasure is scholarly detachment, the truth and goodness that come when we bracket existential commitment to any particular religious tradition, then such scholarly detachment is our religion, the way we've chosen to configure our lives. The fact that the majority of scholars of religion do not claim that historicism or skepticism or de-

tachment is their greatest treasure only suggests that they haven't realized the implications either of their desire to bracket claims to absolute-
ness or uniqueness in their work or of their accepting some such claims
when it comes to their personal lives: what they teach their children,
whether they pray in times of distress or special joy, what they do on the
sabbath, to what they recur when they need to hope that somehow life
does make sense.

When one needs to hope that life makes sense, that the confusion
and darkness, cognitional and moral alike, can be witnesses to the transcendence, the beyond-ness of God, scholarly detachment, historicism,
and the other shibboleths guarding the frontiers of religious studies
against incursions of theology turn out to be pale comfort. The bleak-
ness that was attractive, because it withdrew one from the overheated
claims of many religionists, now seems cold and careless. In fact, historicism then seems to mean relativism of the sort that takes away the
possibility of ultimate significance. If nothing matters absolutely, then
everything may be dismissed.

The Transcendence and Mystery of God

The historicist is leery of making claims that Christ is uniquely
central to salvation or revelation because a full appreciation of time can
seem to relativize all such claims. Each claim comes from a tradition
limited in its experiences, symbols, sense of the full sweep of reality, so
each claim has to be qualified as knowledge advances and the immensity of what the claimers did not know starts to dawn. Underscoring this
immensity, and tying it to religious convictions about the perniciousness of idolatry, another group of present-day scholars concerned to
whittle down past claims for the uniqueness of Christ has focused on
the transcendence and mystery of God. Let us ruminate about their
concerns, which boil down to questioning whether any claim to
uniqueness, in the sense of special adequacy or necessity for the pro-
cesses of salvation and revelation, is compatible with the infinity of the
divine.

The easiest example of the tendency to doubt all human representations of the divine comes from the Abrahamic religions: Judaism,
Christianity, and Islam. Each of these traditions affirms that there is
only one God and that the one God transcends the world. Indeed, the

one God is the creator of the world, its sovereign source. Nothing created can ever capture the truth or goodness or will of the one God, so to place anything created between human beings and the creator is to blaspheme. Idolatry is the serious, perfidious error of letting anything other than God stand for God. Sometimes those who take a position against idolatry realize that they are committing themselves to mysticism, and sometimes they do not. But all who reject finite representations of God imply that mystery, that which is without bounds, has a sacred priority in the way that human beings should configure reality.

Christianity claims to be monotheistic, and so to worship only the one God. Christianity has a tradition of abhorring idolatry and speaking up for the primacy of the divine mystery. Yet Christianity is different from Judaism and Islam, because it confesses the divinity of Jesus Christ. As is clear from the early ecumenical councils, where church leaders gathered to interpret biblical faith and explain Christian convictions, Jesus Christ has been understood to be the incarnation of the self-expression, the Logos, of God. This Logos is everything that the Father, the one to whom Jesus addressed his prayer and other claims upon divinity, is—except that the Father is the source of the Logos and the Logos is the expression of the Father. The full explanation of the Christian understanding of monotheism fills out this description of the relationship between the Logos or Son and the Father by describing the relationship between these two divine "persons" and a third, the Holy Spirit. Christian monotheism therefore is a function of trinitarian theology, according to which the one God is a community (unity is compatible with relational difference).

The more acute issue, however, is the traditional Christian claim that Jesus so incarnated the Logos that Jesus himself should be worshiped as divine. The belief directed toward Jesus has been such that it opened the believer to divinity in a strict sense. This could not mean that the finite became infinite, or that the flesh of Jesus was a mirage. It had to mean that what Jesus most substantially was came from the Logos, actually was the Logos. Certainly this high view of the incarnation was mysterious, as was the constitution of the Trinity and the impartation of divine life called "grace," but those who wished to be orthodox—correct in their praise of God and their thinking about God —confessed it. So the flesh of Jesus functioned as the prime sacrament for the encounter with God. There, in the person, works, and words of Jesus, orthodox Christian believers found divinity most fully revealed.

There they found grace and salvation to be richest. Much of this conviction and commitment was as old as the beginning of the gospel of John: "For the law was given through Moses; grace and truth came through Jesus Christ. No one has ever seen God; the only Son, who is in the bosom of the Father, he has made him known" (Jn 1:17–18).

There are many problems with taking this text as a quick proof that Christianity claims for Jesus the sort of uniqueness flowing from his singular revelation of God and identification with God. Fundamentalism, anti-semitism, and other abuses of texts such as this immediately spring to mind. But abuse should not take away proper use, nor should it dim the apparent, obvious message of the text. Jesus was the early Christians' great source of grace and truth. When one claims that Jesus both is and is not divine, that he is both fully God and fully human, as mainstream, orthodox Christian faith has claimed down through the centuries, one is making a claim with such solid biblical credentials that one can say it was present from the beginning, as soon as there was a Christianity, even though bringing it to articulate clarity understandably took much doing.

How does this view of the divinity of Christ square with the dismissal of Christ's traditionally asserted privileges put forward by scholars such as Wilfred Cantwell Smith, who are anxious to avoid idolatry and trespassing on the mystery of God?[2] Not well. The stumbling block to the Jews that Paul found Jesus to be, and the foolishness to the Gentiles, boil down to the claim that he was divine, the savior of humankind. In addition to their understandable troubles with an incarnational monotheism, many Jews of Paul's day found Jesus' manner of death abhorrent—incompatible with the way a messiah would appear, let alone with the way they understood divinity. The Gentiles Paul had in mind also found crucifixion abhorrent, but what offended them more was the idea that a peasant from a contemptible portion of the empire should be proposed as the enfleshment of the limitless, deathless God. It is hard to see a great difference between the rejections of Christianity brought forward by Jews and Gentiles of Paul's day and the rejections brought forward today in the name of divine transcendence and mystery. Both boggle at the notion of an incarnation, in the full sense of an enfleshment of God justifying our calling Jesus the embodiment of the Logos. Both apparently lack the experience of personal relation with Jesus, taken to be a living Lord, that moves believers to associate salvation—the radical healing of the human condition—with Jesus. Certainly the abuse of this sort of language by fundamentalists should raise cautions. Yet the deeper issue is whether one can keep faith with the cloud of witnesses who have confessed the surpassing significance of Jesus down the ages while withdrawing commitment to his divinity and his personal mediation of salvation.

Do religious studies scholars have to make keeping faith with Christian tradition in this way a criterion of the adequacy of their findings about Jesus? Certainly not. Do Christian theologians and ordinary Christian believers have to manage such a fidelity? We believe they do. Whatever the explanations of the relation between Jesus and other great religious figures Christian theologians eventually manage, unless they have correlated such explanations with the confession of Jesus' divinity and saviorhood echoing in the traditional creeds and spiritual experiences of orthodox Christians, they have abandoned a major portion of their responsibility.

We shall make plain our conviction that attempting such a correlation is a key task incumbent on Christian theologians nowadays. We shall make plain our conviction that God desires the salvation of all people and has not left any group without witnesses to divine grace. And we shall make plain the difficulty of the task of building bridges from traditional Christian convictions to contemporary instincts prompted by awareness of the holiness and vitality one can find among those who are not Christians. At this juncture, however, we are setting the stage by isolating what we take to be the troublesome heart of proposals to retract traditional Christian claims for the uniqueness of Jesus, whether such proposals come from a modern appreciation of historicity or a modern appreciation of divine transcendence. In our view, whatever the provenance, a revision of the image of Jesus that does not encourage believers to go to Jesus as Peter did, for words of everlasting life available nowhere else, does a great disservice. In our view, Christian theology's foremost allegiance should be to the priority of what happened in Jesus Christ, because without such an allegiance one eviscerates the name "Christian."

Social Justice

A third argument for qualifying the traditional Christian claims for the uniqueness of Christ stems from ethics. Because Christian claims for the uniqueness of Christ have played a role in Christians' abuse of other human beings, one should withdraw such claims. A christology intimately tied to systemic patterns of abuse and despite must be rejected as unworthy of both God and healthy human conscience.[3]

Once again, the person sensing that entirely giving up traditional Christian claims for the uniqueness of Christ is disastrous finds this argument knotted. On the one hand, it is true that Christians persecuting Jews or despising native Americans or discriminating against Asians sometimes have offered the uniqueness of their own traditional truth as part of their rationale. On the other hand, does such an abuse take away the rightful use of traditional confessions that no one ever spoke as Jesus had, or that unless Jesus had been united to God as divinity to divinity salvation would not have occurred? In our opinion, the answer should be no, which means that arguments against the uniqueness of Christ drawn from concerns about social justice strike us as tending to throw the baby out with the bath water.

As some of the advocates of such arguments admit, virtually all religious traditions have abused the truths bestowed on them and made such truths grounds for pride, a sense of special election and privilege, and the abuse of people outside their fold. Muslims, Jews, and Buddhists have such sins on their historical record and continue to sin that way today. Even Hindus, who by some accounts are the most tolerant of religionists, bear responsibility for religiously inspired hatred and slaughter. This sad fact does not relieve Christians of the guilt and need for reform that their own crusades, inquisitions, slave-holdings, and the like have created. But it does reconfigure the question about the force of the uniqueness of Christ in the history of human beings' inhumanity to one another.

In our opinion, what we now know about this history counsels all religious traditions to go lightly with, perhaps even to abjure, claims they have made to election. "Election" suggests the biblical, prophetic traditions, whose conceit has been that God spoke to their founders in such a way as to establish unique bonds and make them distinctive, special among all the nations, "the people of God." The problem with such language is that it conflicts with the signs of holiness, and so with closeness to God, flourishing outside of the tradition in question, and that it transfers to the human side of the divine-human relationship honors and dignities rightly belonging only to the divine side.

As many admirable Jewish commentators have pointed out, the election expressed in the Mosaic covenant was not due to any worthiness on Israel's part and should have been understood as more a responsibility toward the nations than something exalting Jews above other peoples. As many admirable Christian commentators have pointed out, the proper attitude for those given the grace of faith is that they have been unprofitable servants, at best only rendering to God what was required of them. Muslim commentators will have to step forward to indicate the analogous calls to humility encoded in the Qur'an, but the basic posture of the devout Muslim bowed low in prayer suggests that these calls are obvious.

In each of these three cases, election or special covenant ought to lead to humility and service rather than arrogance and domination. In each case, those who have despised other people in the name of what they took to be a special status of their own have adulterated the original message. A full study of the dynamics of such adulteration would entail historical, sociological, psychological, economic and no doubt other factors. Often those people seeming most self-important are victims of self-doubt, trying to puff themselves up so they can compete well in a fearsome world. The only point really important for our purposes is the denial that confessing a unique, surpassing value in Christ necessarily leads to feelings of superiority, let alone feelings of contempt for other people. In fact, the more people appreciate the mysteriousness associated with Christ or any other truly holy figure, the more their dispositions are moved toward awe and the confession that God has all the priority. This was the spirit behind Jesus' teaching that his disciples should not judge other people, lest they themselves be judged (by God) and found wanting.

While the bloody history of religious persecutions, many of them to be laid at the doorstep of Christians, provides the backdrop to the ethical arguments advanced against claims for Christ's uniqueness, more recent experiences of injustice and slaughter also have considerable clout. Thus Paul Knitter, linking his desires for interreligious irenicism with perspectives of liberation theologians, can speak movingly about the plight of the poor, the economic and political disenfranchisement of the third world that has some roots in the sense of superiority flourishing in the first world.[4] As noted, the biblical speech about election has been a factor in that sense of superiority, so arguments against election in an abusive sense are arguments for fair treatment of the poor as well as arguments that all native cultures and religious ways deserve a kindly hearing.

For many people fearful of doctrines of election, the Nazi holocaust of Jews and others who did not fit the Nazi sense of Aryan supremacy is an especially horrific lesson. How much Nazism depended on Christianity is a debated question, the general consensus probably being that Christian antisemitism provided considerable background but that Nazism itself was anti-Christian as well as anti-Jewish, as its persecution of many Christians showed. From the Christian side, the witness of such courageous groups as the German Confessing Church makes the case that many Christians realized the antagonism between Hitler and Christ, while the work of some Christians to save Jews and others marked for the death camps adds profound resonance.

Is Christianity, nonetheless, not intrinsically anti-Jewish, inasmuch as the New Testament and Christian origins generally depend on the rejection of the covenant between God and Israel? Does not the foundational Christian sense of the newness and uniqueness of Jesus Christ determine that it will cast off Judaism? These are serious questions, much aired recently, but a fair answering, in our view, makes several important distinctions. First, there is the aspect of Pauline theology that argues for the continuing validity of the law and the covenant with Israel, and that makes Christians debtors to Jews bound to show them humility and gratitude. Second, there is the historical context of a bitter family feud in which Christians and Jews hurled anathemas mutually. Third, and most delicate, there is the Christian sense that Jesus represented a fulfillment of Jewish hopes that many Jews rejected. How culpably they rejected the offer of God that Jesus represented (Jesus' messiahship) is beyond human reckoning, as is any person's ultimate yes or no to God. So Christians erred grievously when they stigmatized Jews as Christ-killers and persecuted them through the centuries. Christians should publicly acknowledge such gross sins of the past and commit themselves to zealous efforts against any repetition. On the other hand, Christians can't be Christians without making Christ their primary allegiance, so it is as unrealistic to ask Christians to give up their traditional confessions about the uniqueness of Christ as it is unrealistic to ask Jews to give up their traditional confessions about the primacy of torah. What is necessary in both cases is a contemporary reinterpretation that delves more deeply into the traditional beliefs and emerges convinced that these beliefs can and should generate humility and social justice, not abort or thwart them.

Wider Perspectives

The arguments against Christian uniqueness, whether they stem from historicist grounds, concerns to avoid idolatry, or worries that traditional christology has fostered social injustice, all bring forward valid fears and difficulties—matters we must continue to address. When one encounters actual adherents of another religious tradition, and finds their humanity admirable, the misconceptions, bigotries, assumptions of superiority, and the like that led one's own tradition to denigrate such people in the past are all revealed to be ugly sins. It becomes clear that God can be no lover of the roots of such sins, because God has to be the lover and source of all people's admirable humanity. So in the name of God one has to criticize the roots of one's tradition's inhumanity and brand them incompatible with authentic Christianity.

It remains true, however, that interreligious dialogue places a pressure on participants to bracket their personal, confessional convictions and move toward something more general, something that all participants, regardless of their confessional ties, can share. Many admirable participants certainly resist this pressure, realizing that the best witness and service they can render is to speak completely honestly, from their existential commitments as Jews or Muslims, Christians or Buddhists. Yet nearly inevitably there is the suggestion that God must be bigger than the confessional perception of God available to people in their religious particularity—the revelations they have as Jews or Muslims, Christians or Buddhists. And, to be frank, there *is* a sense in which all confessions are limiting, all creedal and symbolic systems fail to match the transcendence of God, the omni-relevance of salvation or enlightenment, as the riches one finds outside one's own confessional community manifest. Thus, there is a way in which it is good for people to submit themselves to the generalizing, universalizing tendencies of interreligious dialogue and contemplate the whole drama of humanity's groping toward its source and fulfillment.[5]

For Christians, and no doubt analogously for adherents of other religious traditions, the theological rebound of such dialogical experiences can be a renewed appreciation of how universal and transcendent their traditional God, and their Christ, in fact should seem. In other words, the theological rebound should be a deeper appreciation of the divine mystery, which breaks all the categories we erect for dealing with it, even those most sanctioned by church councils and saints. If the God of Christians, the Trinity confessed throughout Catholic Christian faith, cannot be the light illumining Buddhists or the divinity revealing to Muslims their way, the fault is not with the Trinity but with traditional understandings of it. Inasmuch as interreligious dialogue can disclose such faults, can point out inadequacies in past formulations, interreligious dialogue can be a wonderful source of Christian reform and betterment.

Granted the will to such a reform, however, it remains instructive that nothing brought forward by either the spokespersons of other religious traditions or those who ruminate about the relativities introduced by historicism, the sociology of knowledge, contemporary philosophy, or other hermeneutical studies need move Christians from their conviction that Jesus had and has words of everlasting life to be found nowhere else. The very arguments that cause prudent Christians to be fully aware of the limitations consequent on humanity, whether their own or that of Jesus, free such Christians from fear that Buddhist insights or the insights of historicist theologians can take away their rightful allegiance to Jesus. Nothing need take away that allegiance, assuming that that allegiance expresses the way that given Christians have found the world to make sense, to have a still point that stopped its sickening turning.

When one comes upon a dazzling Buddhist, or Jewish, or Hindu, or Muslim, or other insight, one should simply praise it and try to take it to heart. If it is profound, it will move one into the mystery of God— into the orbit of the Beginning and the Beyond, the One who measures all of human reality and so gives it intelligibility. But one's Christian allegiance takes one to precisely the same place. In fact, if Christianity has been the shaper of one's biographical quest, it is only in virtue of Christian faith and wisdom that one can recognize the profundity and beauty of an insight from another tradition. To be sure, Christian allegiance, as many people actually experience and develop it, can also be a limiting factor—a set of blinders. But it is not hard to argue that this is another instance of abuse, of inauthentic Christian faith. Other traditions no doubt have the need and right to make the same claim: prejudice, limitation, having been closed are marks of inauthentic Buddhist, Jewish, Hindu, Muslim, or other allegiance. Each tradition will have to work out its own analysis of what is necessary for it to be a definite something, a tradition with a particular identity, and what is an inauthentic limiting or crippling, but at first blush it certainly would seem possible to argue that what genuine engagement with the path laid out by torah or Muhammad or the Buddha or Hindu dharma (teaching) involves is always capable of expanding one's capacities, is always transcendent in the sense of reaching out toward the limitless beyond, the inexhaustible godhead, in which or in whom one may hope to find all apparent oppositions reconciled.

So, the more that the rebound or recoil from interreligious dialogue moves Christians to reexamine their sense of God and Christ, the more likely Christians are to deepen their appreciation of what such traditional words as "divine" and "infinite," "transcendent" and "saving," properly denote. None of these words is tame. None is the captive of human understanding. Each most rightfully arose from experiences of the limitlessness of the wisdom and goodness revealed in Jesus and connoted by "Father," "Logos," and "Spirit." Thus, interreligious dialogue should never cause the committed and mature Christian believer to doubt the adequacy of Christ. Virtually by definition, Christ the God-man can handle whatever new insight or challenge to old formulations or practices interreligious dialogue can muster.

In saying this we are not trying to remove the shock of having one's traditional formulations or understandings challenged. Such a shock can be salutary in the extreme, for it can reveal not only the bigotry or sin in one's past tradition or self but also the richness of one's God and Christ that hitherto one had not appreciated. Moreover, the existential stance, associated with spirituality, that we have stressed provides another legitimate, nearly inevitable buffer and consolation. Every interlocutor one meets in interreligious dialogue, whether around a table or through books, is going to die, is ignorant, and has sinned. All have fallen short of the glory of God and none has ever seen God face to face. Balancing this with the imperatives of one's own life, which are summarily to find a way to make it through the day, a way that will give enough light and warmth to call life good, one can easily take much of the rhetoric that apologists for interreligious dialogue indulge with a grain of salt. Not only is interreligious dialogue not going to furnish a panacea or substitute for living religious faith, it is also not going to remove the deep conviction of any mature Christian believer that Peter's confession of the uniqueness of Christ expresses a perennial truth. Because such a conviction has been forged in spiritual passion—dark nights and clouds of unknowing when the preciousness of Christ's sacramentality was seared into one's soul—nothing so fragile as the words, the ideas, even the winning warmth of one's dialogical partners, who are all fellow mortals, is likely to trouble mature believers seriously. Even less likely to trouble them are the adversarial views of people whose existential reasons for proposing the demise of the uniqueness of Christ have not been laid out on the table and remain suspect as not having been forged in fires of similar spiritual intensity.

NOTES

1. Gordon D. Kaufman, "Religious Diversity, Historical Consciousness, and Christian Theology," in THE MYTH OF CHRISTIAN UNIQUENESS, eds. John Hick and Paul F. Knitter (Maryknoll, N.Y.: Orbis, 1987), p. 9. See also the studies by John Hick and Langdon Gilkey in that volume.

2. See Wilfred Cantwell Smith, "Idolatry: In Comparative Perspective," ibid., pp. 53–68, as well as the studies by Stanley J. Samartha, Raimundo Panikkar, and Seiichi Yagi in the same volume.

3. See Tom F. Driver, CHRIST IN A CHANGING WORLD (New York: Crossroad, 1981), as well as the studies by Rosemary Radford Ruether, Marjorie Hewitt Suchocki, Aloysius Pieris, and Paul F. Knitter in THE MYTH OF CHRISTIAN UNIQUENESS.

4. See Paul F. Knitter, "Toward a Liberation Theology of Religions," in THE MYTH OF CHRISTIAN UNIQUENESS, pp. 178–200; also his contribution to a symposium reviewing Jon Sobrino's SPIRITUALITY OF LIBERATION, HORIZONS, 16/1 (Spring 1989), 131–135.

5. See Leonard Swidler, ed., TOWARD A UNIVERSAL THEOLOGY OF RELIGION (Maryknoll, N.Y.: Orbis, 1987).

Chapter 3

How Christ Is Not Unique

Religious Diversity

We begin our appreciation of the good reasons behind many proposals to reexamine traditional expressions of Christian conviction about the uniqueness of Christ by contemplating the world's religious diversity. A good start is simply to bring forward representative figures about the various allegiances that the present five billion or so inhabitants of our earth display. There are about 1,670 million Christians, 881 million Muslims, 664 million Hindus, 312 million Buddhists, 172 million Chinese folk religionists (Taoists/Confucians), 112 million adherents of Asian "New Religions," 92 million adherents of tribal religions, 18 million Jews, 17 million Sikhs, 6 million Confucians (mainly Korean), 4.7 million Baha'is, 3.5 million Jains, and 3.4 million adherents of Shinto. About 867 million people can be considered nonreligious, about 230 million are atheists, about 12 million adhere to shamanic traditions different from Chinese folk religion or the tribal religions of other lands (e.g., Africa), and about 8 million people adhere to smaller religious groups.[1]

The classifications used in this survey to group both adherents of religion and those refusing allegiance to any religion are open to considerable criticism, as are the numbers entered for each tradition, but the survey and statistics are representative. It is interesting that virtually one of every three people is accounted a Christian (32.9 percent), that Roman Catholics constitute the largest individual bloc (952 million), that Christians are found in all 254 countries surveyed, and that Muslims and nonreligious people are nearly equal in number: 881 million to 867 million. These data are for the year 1988, and of course they keep changing. Christians and Muslims are the groups growing most rapidly.

33

More than three-quarters of the nonreligious people (664 million of 867 million) are in East Asia, while East Asians provide about 60 percent of those labeled atheists (140 million of 230 million). The Soviet Union provides more than 25 percent of the world's atheists (60 million of 230 million). Christians are the largest religious body in six of the eight continental areas the survey uses: Africa, Europe, Latin America, Northern America, Oceania, and the USSR. Only in East Asia, where nonreligious people, Chinese folk religionists, Buddhists, and atheists have greater numbers, and in South Asia, where Hindus, Muslims, and Buddhists have greater numbers, are Christians not the largest group. Even there, however, Christian numbers are impressive: 82 million in East Asia and 132 million in South Asia.

Our point certainly is not to brag about Christian missionary accomplishments, though it is instructive to realize just how catholic (universal) Christianity has become. Our point rather is to appreciate the diversity of the ways that people are trying to fashion meaningful pathways through space and time and correlate that diversity with Christian convictions about the universality of divine grace. The vast majority of the world's people, more than 75 percent, apparently are religious in some mode. Nonreligious and atheistic people number a daunting population (about 1,110 million), but almost 4,000 million people are religious. Christians are more than 40 percent of these religious people (1,670 million). The major partners for dialogue that Christians should seek out, if numbers be their guide, are nonreligious people, Muslims, Hindus, Buddhists, and atheists. East Asia is the place for dialogue with nonreligious people and atheists. South Asia is the place for dialogue with Muslims and Hindus. Buddhists are nearly equally populous in East Asia and South Asia. Europe has about 53 million nonreligious people and 18 million atheists, while the USSR has about 86 million nonreligious people and about 61 million atheists.

Beneath these statistics of course thrives much greater diversity. People have nearly as many different ways of being nonreligious, atheistic, Muslim, Hindu, Buddhist, and Christian as they have different names, noses, and walks. What they hold in common as members of a validly demarcated group is significant, but many subdivisions, sects, and secondary traditions give their lives spice and color. Christians, for example, number about 952 million Roman Catholics, 337 million Protestants, 162 million Orthodox, 70 million Anglicans, and 148 million who fall outside these four categories. About 83 percent of the world's Muslims are Sunnis and about 16 percent are Shiites. About 70 percent of the world's Hindus are Vaishnavites (devotees of Vishnu/Krishna) and about 25 percent are Shaivites (devotees of Shiva). About 56 percent of the world's Buddhists are Mahayanists, about 38 percent are Theravadins, and about six percent are Tantrists.

So there is much diversity within each of the major religious traditions—so much that many scholars consider each tradition more an umbrella than a decisive designation. In thinking about this diversity, Christians do well to focus on all three aspects of the trinitarian God whom they confess. First, in each human being's life there is more to know than the person ever masters and so there is great mystery. Indeed, this mystery is qualitative more than quantitative: what it is most imperative that people know, if they are to understand their human condition, is their Beginning and Beyond, which they can never know, at least not as items of information. But Christianity has long associated such fontal, aboriginal mystery with the divine Father, who has stood in the best sketches of the trinitarian relations as the underived source of derivation, the unbegotten source of origination. Although creation has traditionally been attributed to the Trinity as a whole, making it a work of God as one or the three "persons" as united, within the Trinity the Father has been considered the (beginningless) beginning. So it is logical for Christian faith to implicate the Father in the depths of each person's and tradition's wrestlings with the mystery of Beginning and Beyond. It is logical for Christians to think of the Father when they ponder the scriptural saying that God has not left divinity without trace anywhere.

The Son/Logos has long been associated with the intelligibility of creation, in reflection of his procession from the Father as the Father's self-expression. The Father, knowing himself, expresses that knowing, that self, as the Son/Logos. Inasmuch as creation occurs as a function of the trinitarian constitution of the one God, it makes sense to correlate the intelligibility of creation with the Son/Logos (Word, second person). It is he in whom the Pauline school found all creation to hold together. It is through him that the Johannine school considered all things to have come to be. The relatively new theory that creation is chaotic, or has an intrinsic element of chaos, may be handled by saying that this chaos is order to the mind of God, and so is expressed in the

Logos, who is infinite. Whether there can be irrationality, disorder, in divinity is a challenging question, but the weight of Christian tradition is to say no: God is light, in whom there is no darkness at all. What is darkness to human beings can be light to God. Indeed, God regularly appears to human beings as darkness, so much so that darkness is a commonplace in mystical literature.

Third, we may associate the affectivity, ardor, and spiritual move-ment displayed so variously by the different religious, and nonreligious, traditions with the Holy Spirit. Whenever people move toward the good, the beautiful, what is right, they do so, for Christian faith, under the impulse of the divine Spirit. Within the Trinity the Spirit is the love breathed forth by Father and Son in their mutual knowing. In human beings' relationship with God, the Spirit pours forth heartfelt love as an expression of God's having both given divine life and caused divine life to be received. The Spirit's movement has something round or holistic about it, such that it makes sense to picture the Spirit brooding over the waters of creation, making the Beginning inspire existence in time, as well as to picture the Spirit guiding all of history, cosmic and human alike, to its consummation in God.

So the more one contemplates with Christian faith the diversity of people's ultimately human, religious experience, the more one finds witness to the constant presence and work of the Trinity. Religious diversity suggests that Christ is not unique in having inspired people to seek the mystery holding their lives, however much Christian faith may think that Christ's inspiration best expresses how such seeking occurs ideally. If people everywhere may be interpreted as involved with the Trinity, then the specifically Christian line of history is not the only channel of grace. That, in turn, suggests that Jesus Christ is not the only means of revelation that God has used, though it leaves open the ques-tion of the relation between Jesus and other means of revelation. As well, it leaves open the possibility that the revelation given through Jesus Christ might have some theological priority, such that one could say that other revelations are best understood as having occurred in virtue of Jesus Christ. Jesus Christ then might seem the exemplary cause of such other revelations—the personal pattern best illumining their full implications. But speculation such as this is best reserved for later chapters. Sufficient for the moment is a faithful appreciation of the fact that the God whom Christians worship may be believed to have long been at work in non-Christian religions, as well as in the aspirations of nonreligious people toward truth and love.

Limitations on Christianity

The upshot of any representative statistical overview of today's global religious situation is that Jesus Christ has not been the only inspiration of religious conviction and activity. This is a minimal conclusion, occurring at some distance from the central revisions of traditional Christian ideas about the uniqueness of Christ that some contemporary reformers desire, but it is suggestive. When we ask why God should have used channels of revelation other than Jesus Christ and Christianity, we naturally run into the mysteriousness of creation and providence. Nonetheless, some insight comes when we think about the consequences of finitude, space, and time. The divine decision to communicate existence to rational creatures limited by bodies made it likely, though not certain, that the love affair God wanted to establish with such creatures would take on many different forms and colors.

The limitations of Christianity that first spring to mind derive from human finitude. If Christianity were to begin at a specific intersection of space and time, the portion of God's love affair that went before it would have to be non-Christian (or pre-Christian). Similarly, the portion of God's love affair that went on in other geographical areas would have to be non-Christian (or pre-Christian). Thus God can be seen as having chosen, for God's own good purposes, to vary the modes of the divine love affair with human beings (divinization). God can be seen as having chosen to limit the range and in some ways the significance of the explicitly Christian channels of grace.

Further, to be fully human Jesus Christ had to suffer most of the limitations that afflict all other members of the human race. He could not stand apart as not needing food, not needing rest, knowing everything, being immortal, succeeding in his every endeavor. He had to move through his lifetime with a sense that the future was open-ended and his decisions were significant. He had to be liable to sorrow and disappointment, as well as joy and fulfillment. These are the straightforward deductions of the traditional, orthodox Christian teaching about the full humanity of Christ. Simply by explicating them, one finds myriad ways in which Christ was limited and Christ was not unique.

Ah, but what about Christ's divinity, which has been an equally traditional, orthodox teaching? Is Jesus Christ not unique in having been, in the strictest sense, the Son of God—light from light, true God from true God? Yes, Christian faith has to say he has been uniquely divine, if it is to maintain communion with the orthodoxy taught and lived down the ages from the New Testament era. Still, how to correlate the humanity and divinity of Christ has always been a baffling task, and what the implications of such a correlation ought to be for thinking about the comparison of Christ with other religious founders and saints admits of much debate, as present-day discussions such as the one we have joined demonstrate.

How to correlate the humanity and divinity of Christ is a baffling task because one is trying to square a circle. The circle is divinity, which never ends (and actually has no circumferential limits). The square is humanity, which by comparison seems well defined (but in fact is also mysterious, since the human spirit moves toward transcendence—more and more light and love). It is easier to say what the intimate, completely integral union of humanity and divinity in Jesus Christ did not produce, and then what it did produce, than to say how it works. It did not produce any limitation on Christ's divinity, because divinity is not limited (though possibly divinity does limit itself, in ways we cannot imagine, when it creates [makes finite beings], or divinizes [makes rational creatures partakers of its deathless love], or [most acutely] unites itself substantially or personally [hypostatically] with a full human being, as it did uniquely [traditional Christian faith says] in the case of Jesus Christ).

The incarnation did not produce any confusion of divinity and humanity, because that would have blurred the unblurrable and been, with special accent on the divine side of Christ's reality, a source of idolatry. If Christ were not fully divine, then to worship him would have been idolatrous. But Christ was worshiped from the outset of Christian faith. Therefore the deepest instinct of Christian faith was that he was divine—such was the reasoning of the councils and fathers who paved the way to Nicaea and Chalcedon, the ecumenical meetings that formalized traditional faith about Jesus Christ. The actual evolution of what became the classical articulation of traditional faith was nothing so syllogistic as the way we have just expressed it, yet basically that was the logic.

The incarnation could not have removed anything essential to Christ's full humanity, because then it would not have been a genuine, complete incarnation—a "taking flesh" that made the Logos the ultimate source of the act of existence of a thoroughly human being. As the traditional practice of worshiping Christ shaped the conviction that he was unconfusedly divine, so the traditional convictions about salvation shaped the confessions of Christ's full humanity: what was not assumed was not saved. For humanity to have been saved in the radical way that believers' experience of Christ said it had been saved, Jesus had to have been "like us in all things save sin." He had to be one of us, a complete fellow member of our race. This was one "explanation" of his having suffered and died. To restructure things in the radical way that Christian instinct said God had restructured them in Christ (the Pauline "new creation"), the divine plan of salvation went to depths of human need and overcame our mortality and vulnerability, making the fact that we die and can suffer ways of transforming us into sharers of God's deathless, beatific existence. Of course Christians, and any others taking on these propositions, have only been able to stutter about them, because they bear on actions of an agent we cannot understand. But in all their stuttering the orthodox were guided and stabilized by the conviction that the full humanity of Jesus was essential to the process of salvation.

More positively, one can say that the union of divinity and humanity in Christ produced a perfected human being. Because his union with his Father took Jesus to the peak of human fulfillment, bringing him to the consummation postulated by his human spiritual dynamics, Jesus Christ was a revelation of human potential, as well as a revelation of what divinity is like in human terms. Moreover, inasmuch as his union with divinity required and caused his sinlessness, his humanity was uniquely unfettered by the bad choices, the selfishness, the lovelessness, the malice that fetter other human beings. The early Christians were so impressed by what Jesus had accomplished—salvation, as most dramatically evidenced by the resurrection—that they inferred such a perfection, or lack of imperfection (sin), in his makeup. Their memories of how Jesus looked, spoke, acted, prayed, loved, and the rest also contributed to this conclusion that he was uniquely unflawed—had and was the words of everlasting life.

All of this anticipates what, in our view, Christian theologians ought to be safeguarding when they discourse about the implications of interreligious dialogue for contemporary Catholic spirituality. On the other hand, it brings forward the primary ways in which Christ was not unique—all that he shared with his fellow human beings—and helps us position Christianity properly humbly for interreligious dialogue. First, Christianity, as the tradition descended from Jesus, has been liable to the same vicissitudes of space and time that other human traditions have (and these vicissitudes are providential, in the sense of implied in creation). Second, Christianity has to recur to faith, interpreting the humanity and divinity of Jesus in committed love, if it is to reach its traditional christological conclusions. This faith is a limitation, in the sense that people who do not share it cannot see the divinity and humanity of Jesus Christ in the same light. Third, Christians can never fully explain their faithful estimates of Jesus, including their estimates of his uniqueness, because even with faith the nexus between the divinity and the humanity of Jesus Christ remains strictly mysterious: a function of the ungraspable being, will, and action of God.

Plurality

In some recent treatments of the foundations of a properly contemporary christology the question of plurality assumes great philosophical significance.[2] Not only must one contend with the plurality of saviors and divinities promoted by the world religions, one must also contend with the proposition that at bottom the world is many, not one. This latter proposition conflicts with the instinct of most traditional western thought, and much traditional eastern thought. Generally, the religious traditions, west and east, have assumed that God, the ultimate reality, had to be One, and that being, the existence dependent on God, had to be one more ultimately than it was many. Two significant challenges to this general assumption were mainstream Buddhist thought, which tended to say that ultimate reality was neither one nor many, and Christian trinitarian theology, which made divinity a dynamic tension of unity and relational difference. Mainstream Buddhist thought denied the ability of human intelligence to capture ultimate reality in any positive way, sensing a fallacy in the tendency (prominent in Hinduism) to imagine a monistic ultimate reality (Brahman) underlying the phenomena revealed to human experience. Keeping faith with the Buddha's reluctance to speak about ultimate reality, which probably implied a profound appreciation of how ultimate reality is always the source of our linguistic categories and never their captive, Buddhist philosophers tended to approach metaphysical questions dialectically, denying both affirmations and negations put forward about ultimate reality (*nirvana*). For example, they would say that nirvana is neither light nor not-light, neither being nor non-being. Inasmuch as they were also reluctant to separate ultimate reality from fleeting, insubstantial, painful daily reality (*samsara*), they painted a picture (or a nonpicture) in which ultimate reality could be identified with the multiplicity of things, thoughts, sensations, and the like that seem to constitute the field of awareness and reality.

Christian trinitarian theology never made the impact on the Greek metaphysics inherited and used by those who first developed the speculative side of Christian faith that one might have expected. It did not, for instance, create the nuance about the priority of unity over plurality that one could have expected, had one let the Christian symbol of the Trinity direct one's thinking about the creatures made in the likeness of the Trinity. Thus there was little imagery for how the source of meaning postulated by the world's plurality, change, and diversity (signs that the world, as finite, did not supply its own source of meaning) might be a unity in tension with relational difference, as the Trinity was. To be sure, at the outer edges of theological creativity, where the tools that theologians had inherited from their cultural traditions were shaping, and being shaped by, instincts of faith (generated by the byplay between the Bible and the Holy Spirit in believers' minds and hearts), what the Trinity itself could mean was up for grabs. The best speculators remained well aware that they were better at saying what the Trinity apparently could not be (because a given hypothesis violated other tenets of Christian faith or ran counter to human rationality) than what it was positively. Working quite gingerly, they could say, for example, that the Father, Son, and Spirit could not be distinct really, because that would make them three different Gods, which was counter to faith (and Hellenistic metaphysics). Thus, the distinctions among the divine persons had to be rooted in their relations, in such wise that the Son was not the Father only because the Son was the generated and not the generator. Similarly, the Spirit was not the Father or the Son because the Spirit was the spirated and the Father and Son were the spirators. Generation and spiration were metaphors, of course, as the best theologians realized, But they were metaphors with canonical status, because they were suggested by scripture and had been used by the most revered early Christian theologians to probe the divine mystery into which scripture led.

Perhaps significantly, eastern Christianity showed a stronger predilection for the pluralistic side of the Trinity than did western Christianity, so the eastern liturgy was richer with allusions to the operations of the different divine persons. In the west the Trinity was confessed as a key portion of the creed, but most western piety was trinitarian only weakly or implicitly. For both the east and the west, it was impossible to separate trinitarian questions from christological ones, especially when one was dealing with the liturgy and devotional matters. When one focused on Jesus Christ, one quickly became immersed in his primary relationships, which were with his Father and Spirit.

At any rate, little in Christian theology, west or east, brought to bear on non-Christian religions such pluralism as christology, bound to trinitarian theology, suggested. Further, little contested the instinct that what God had done in Christ (revelation and salvation alike) had been done once and for all. The uniqueness and adequacy of God's revelation and salvation in Christ stood virtually unquestioned. These were clear from scripture (Rom 6:10; Heb 7:27; 9:12; 9:26; 10:10; 1 Pet 3:18), and Christian instinct felt that all human beings were invited into the riches of God's mercy offered in Christ. That was the great imperative behind the missionary activity that galvanized the Christian community from the beginning. Extending the notion of good news prominent in Jesus' own preaching, the early Christian missionaries made the fullness of the good news the fact, as they saw it, that Christ had died, once, and for all sinners (all human beings), making possible all people's reconcilation with God and one another. Any pluralism of salvation would amount to a diversity of ways of appropriating this decisive, eschatological (definitive) action of God in Christ.

Is this traditional christological and soteriological (salvational) conviction set aside when present-day Christian revisionists seek to place Jesus more on a par with other religious founders and soteriological figures than in a place and importance all his own? Yes, apparently so. If the people equalizing the importance of Christ and other great religious figures, such as the Buddha and Muhammad, are claiming to be working as theologians, rather than as comparative religionists, they would seem to be setting traditional christological faith aside. Theologians propose fresh understandings of traditional symbols of faith. Comparative religionists can set aside the faith of any particular tradition, using only scholarly analysis as their interpretational horizon, so that they let given figures be only what their followers claim them to be. In our present case, that could mean that the Buddha, Muhammad, and Christ are all equal, because followers of each claim to have found salvation in them or their message.

Christian theologians, it would seem, may not reduce Christ to the equal of other soteriological figures without departing from the canonical symbols of Christian faith and the long-standing orthodox understanding of such symbols. They may not take away the once and for all of the Christ event, the early Christian sense that God had reconciled the world to divinity in the death and resurrection of Christ, without venturing into something novel and probably diminished. They may notice the perhaps parallel claims of Buddhists, Muslims, and other religionists, as they may notice the denial by such other religionists that Christ should have such a signal status. But Christian theologians cannot make such parallel claims equal to Christian claims without twisting the faith handed down to them, and they cannot accept other religionists' denials of Christ's signal status without withdrawing their allegiance from Jesus. They can be pluralistic in their attempts to explain what the saving work of Jesus might mean for non-Christians, and they can be pluralistic in their estimates of the significance or value of the Buddha, Muhammad, and other great religious figures. Finally, they certainly can diverge in their judgments about the most politic way to represent Christian convictions when in dialogue with non-Christians.

A Comparative Perspective on Idolatry

We have mentioned the Buddhist instinct that ultimate reality is beyond description, either positive or negative. Similar instincts appear in most other religious traditions. Generally, significant religious traditions arise from profound, truly religious experiences in which a sensitive person directly encounters the divine or ultimate and is changed forever. The biographies of Moses, Muhammad, and the Buddha reflect some such experience, and even though the textual sources do not permit an exact understanding of what happened to any of these three figures, they suggest that the person realized, beyond doubt or cavil, that the realest thing in the world was not a thing and could not be comprehended ("grasped"). Moses, drawn by the burning bush, soon learned that the holy ground on which he had ventured got its consecration from the presence of One who could never surrender his name (the manipulation of him) into the control of human beings. YHWH, the consonantal term given to the Lord, was not uttered by the pious, as a sign of their understanding the transcendence, the holy distance, of the Master of the Universe. Moses learned only that the One whom he had experienced wanted to call Moses' people into convenantal relationship—wanted to make a pact, according to which he (the patriarchal society of Moses' time determined that divinity would receive mainly masculine linguistic forms) and they would go through time together. The Lord would always be mysterious, sovereignly free of human control, because that was his nature—that was what being God was bound to imply, when one cashed it out in human terms.

Muhammad, gone out into the desert night to meditate about the meaning of life, received visions of a shining figure, later thought to be the angel Gabriel, who commanded him to recite—proclaim—a message about the soleness, the unicity, of Allah. Thus, the first expression of Muslim faith became the confession that there is no god but God, and that Muhammad is God's (Allah's) prophet. The worst sin in the Muslim catalogue is unbelief, and the major manifestation of unbelief is idolatry: associating anything with Allah, obscuring in any way the priority and exhaustiveness of the claim of Allah upon the allegiance, the heart, of the human being. Allah is the Lord of the Worlds, the sole reason that anything came to be. Obscuring this truth in any way made one a menace, because it made one a disturber of the order necessary if praise and service of Allah were to flourish. Only from the flourishing of the praise and service of Allah could human beings expect to find political order: peace and prosperity. Only from such right religion, right ultimate allegiance, could they expect to gain cultural cohesion: meaning, beauty, dignity. So it was imperative to fight idolatry on all sides, constantly defending faith against encroachments upon the soleness of Allah, against rivals to Allah's exclusive and exhaustive claim upon human allegiance.

The Buddha also knew that no human speech could capture the essence of what is most real and important. As well, he also knew that the human craving for more tangible, less ultimate sources of pleasure and security was a constant danger to right human order. So the Buddha prohibited discussions of ultimate reality, urging people to seek the experience rather than the mere language, and he urged his followers to root out the desire for anything other than the ungraspable ultimate reality itself. Since this ultimate reality was not a thing, not a substance, not ultimate as the last item in a chain of finite entities or reasons, it wasn't "ultimate" in the way that the human imagination and reason tended to present it. It was primary, as much as ultimate. It was present, immanent, as much as beyond. And it "was" the total circuit of beings, in their causal relationships, as much as something other than or beyond this circuit. It was not nameable and it was not not nameable. It was unique, and people better approached it through silent attention (meditation) than through anything wordy or busy.

These three examples of the relation between a profound religious experience and the conviction that nothing can adequately represent divinity or reality at its most real suggest a comparative appreciation of idolatry. As soon as human beings get a taste of the living God, they become sensitive to the omnipresence and virulence of false gods. False gods are any objects of passionate, profound human devotion that claim to be ultimate and are not, because they do not hand one over into the strict mysteriousness of the truly divine. Because they attempt to draw ultimate human concern to themselves, they try to distort the human makeup and are bound to deliver only disappointment and disarray. The human heart will not be mocked. When something not truly ultimate tries to supply for God, the result is ashes, wormwood, gall and bile. Only the truly ultimate can give the human spirit the freedom and joy it craves. Whenever the human spirit finds its thrust of mind and heart toward the whole, the exhaustive, the really ultimate and explanatory good thwarted or frustrated, it knows it has met something inimical to true religion and full humanity. The fact that many such barriers have been erected by religious institutions only underscores the perniciousness of idolatry. In the name of the real God, the truly ultimate good, people often have to fight against the supposed guardians of religion, the teachers supposed to show the way that is straight and true.

Jesus' exemplification of this sort of insight into idolatry was rich and unique. For although one can say that the Buddha, the Qur'an, and the torah hold in their respective religious traditions places analogous to the place held by the Incarnate Word in the Christian configuration of reality, each of these other centers points away from itself differently from the way that Christian faith has pointed away from Jesus and to the Father who for Jesus was the living God. The Buddha was the Enlightened One, and later many of his followers (especially those worshiping in Mahayana and Vajrayana [tantric] forms) treated him as a divinity. But the ultimacy that the Buddha (Gautama, the historical man) concentrated upon was something revealed to him in meditation and open to any who replicated his meditational experience. It was tied intimately to his exemplary personal experience, but one may question whether it was as inseparable from his reality as was the ultimacy, the divinity, that Christian faith has discovered in Jesus. As early as the gospel of John, and perhaps in the writings of Paul and the synoptics (which most scholars consider earlier than John), Jesus appears to be so identified with his Father ("I and the Father are one" [Jn 10:30]) as to warrant the later expression "consubstantial" (possessing the same substance, being the same in order, kind, and number).

This view of Jesus depends on the passionate love we have associated with faith, which certainly has parallels in the Buddhist regard of Gautama. The passionate love that Muslims have showered upon the Qur'an and Jews have showered upon torah is somewhat similar, though obviously neither the Qur'an nor the torah is personal as Jesus and the Buddha are. (Muslims have always denied the divinity of Muhammad, as Jews have denied any divinity to Moses.)

What is unique about the Christian efforts to articulate true divinity and, relatedly, a proper view of idolatry is the incarnational conviction consequent on the Christian identification of Jesus and the Father. Whether or not this would be perceptible to those outside Christian faith or working in the comparative horizon proper to religious studies, from within Christian faith it was not only not idolatrous to worship Jesus as divine, it was requisite to worship him as divine. When Christians confessed that they believed in Jesus Christ, the only Son, their Lord, they offered to Christ latria, the sort of devotion (true worship) due only to the living God, the transcendent Holy One. Because of their commitment to the Trinity, they further believed that this worship of Christ took them toward Father, Son, and Spirit. In worshiping Christ, they were entering the trinitarian relations, in the sense that the divine life given them in faith had the "structure" of placing them "in" the Son (Paul's "in Christ"). This meant that their prayer ascended to the Father, orientation to whom was the Son's complete desire, and that the Spirit of the Father and the Son moved in their hearts, as it had moved in the heart of Jesus. So, the worship of the God-man moved "through" the symbolic reality of Jesus Christ as through a lens and reached out to the sole God, living and true. The lens purified and sharpened this worship, rather than distorting it (as anything idolatrous would). In the Son, through the movement of the Spirit, Christians offered the worship proper to what the living Godhead had shown itself to be: a community of light and love originating from the Father. Jesus avoided all idolatry by setting his heart only on the Father, and Jesus avoided calling himself divine because, granted the linguistic usages of his day, that probably would have confused him with the Father. By the time that the author of the gospel of John was construing christology, however, it had become clear that, without ceasing to be human and the Father's Son, Jesus Christ was one with the Father: very God of very God. He was the icon of the Father, the perfect image and representation, so directing worship to the Father through him was meet and just, proper and helpful unto salvation.

Christ in Comparative Perspective

On the basis of what we have seen thus far, one might conclude that only the Buddha seems comparable with Jesus as a locus of worship. With a few qualifications (the devotional response of some Muslims to Muhammad has approached worship, the Hindu worship of the mythic figure Krishna has borne affinities to the love Christians have lavished upon Christ, the Virgin Mary has functioned for some Christians as a goddess), this conclusion seems warranted. Certainly, Buddhism is the closest parallel to the Christian tendency to merge the career and person of an historical figure with the appearance of ultimate reality, the truly divine, for the sake of salvation.

On examination, however, one notes the differences already suggested between the Buddha and Jesus, as well as the richer overtones to the Christian understanding of "history." To an outsider, the identification between Gautama and the reality he perceived in enlightenment seems less personal, consubstantial, hypostatic than what Christian believers confess to be the case with Christ. The early Buddhist scriptures certainly identify the career of the Buddha with the arrival of salvation, in the sense of a definitive solution to the problem of suffering. But it is only when Buddhism becomes more metaphysical and worshipful, in the development of Mahayana, that the identification between the being of Gautama and the principle of the world's intelligibility (buddha-nature, suchness, Dharmakaya) begins to parallel the Christian view of the incarnation of the divine Logos in Jesus the Christ. Certainly there are questions about the development of the Christian doctrine of the Logos, and certainly the reading of the Christ of the synoptic gospels that makes him divine in an ontological way (in his being) is usually eisegetical: imports perspectives of faith only clarified after the time of the synoptic gospels. But the flesh of Christ still seems more sacramental, more iconic, more the medium of revelation and salvation than what Buddhists claim for the flesh of the Buddha. Perhaps for that reason, much Mahayana devotion finally abandoned the historical Buddha, multiplied Buddhas, and permitted such sayings as the Zen counsel to "slay" the Buddha (drop reliance on him and find enlightenment in oneself).

It would be understandable, however, if the sorts of distinctions we have been making in this comparison of Christ and the Buddha bothered religious studies scholars. First, we have been working from inside Christian faith and outside Buddhist commitment, making it easy to question the parity of our descriptions. And, second, our interpretations of Jesus have depended on accepting the spirituality inculcated by the New Testament, the church councils, and later tradition. To one looking at Christianity from the outside, our views might seem only one possible interpretation of Christian faith in Jesus (an interpretation stressing "high" christology, while many Christian theologians hold "low" christologies). As well, the Buddha, Krishna, Muhammad, and perhaps other figures might seem quite the equal of Jesus functionally: in the role they played mediating salvation.

This possible, indeed probable, dissonance that many dealing comparatively with Christ could hear illustrates the heart of the problematic of interreligious dialogue. One is always trying to represent one's own tradition as both an insider and an outsider, while trying as an outsider to grasp the insider's view of another tradition. Thus at least four different viewpoints are at work in any serious comparison, and even if one is sophisticated enough to keep the four different interpretational horizons distinguished, the relationship among them is bound to be confusing. Can one be both insider and outsider to one's own faith, let alone the faith of other religionists? At what point does one have to limit one's interpretational ambitions and settle for removing misunderstandings—other people's apparent misunderstandings of one's own tradition, and one's own apparent misunderstandings of other people's traditions? Without denying that any progress in mutual understanding is precious, or even that it is a valid aim of interreligious dialogue to make all participants admirers of one another's heroes and values, it would seem inevitable that the foremost task of interreligious dialogue, because the most practical, should be to reach agreement on such actionable matters as removing discrimination and bigotry, increasing political equality, and banding together to fight such common enemies as environmental pollution.

If this estimate of interreligious dialogue rings true, then the universalism sought by some experienced dialoguers comes into question.[3] The responsibility of presenting one's own religious convictions, presumably rooted in the orthodoxy of one's own tradition, bulks large, and expressions of a desire to be faithful to the canonical expressions of one's own tradition—for example, to the classical formulations of christology rooted in Nicaea and Chalcedon—become highly desirable, perhaps even required.[4] One becomes no less obligated to hear what other religionists are saying, by opening one's mind and heart, but one accepts the pluralism of humanity's ways to ultimate reality as virtually incapable of removal. Inevitable, as well, become one's efforts to interpret the phenomena pointed to by other people's traditions in terms of one's own basic commitments—for example, to interpret the Buddha in terms of the universal salvation one finds in Christ. One may admire the plasticity of fellow Christians who claim to be both Buddhists and Christians, yet wonder about the reality of this claimed achievement— wonder whether it can be squared with the orthodox Christian claims for Jesus. If being a Christian means making Christ the lancet of one's interpretation of all significant phenomena, how can one do justice to claims from inside Buddhist faith? Jesus said that no person can serve two masters. Has interreligious dialogue managed to overcome this saying? If so, hasn't it replaced Christ with a higher hermeneutical authority and so caused those who accept such higher authority to cease to be Christians—people whose first allegiance, whose true worship, pours out to Christ?

In comparative perspective, Christ remains a scandal. The Christian proposition that the power unleashed in nuclear explosions, the power responsible for the big bang that launched the universe, tabernacled uniquely in Jesus of Nazareth boggles the mind as much as the mathematics of such power do. Quite literally, we cannot get the human mind around the most central proposition of Christian faith: the full humanity and full divinity of Jesus the Christ. What measure of intelligibility one can find in that proposition is more the work of the heart than the work of the mind. One doesn't believe it precisely because it is absurd, but one does have to reckon with the superrational character of one's belief. It may seem strangely fitting, congruent with the divine goodness, that divinity should have found a way to unite itself so intimately with us human beings and our salvation, but it always remains a shock to live faith. For live faith, God is never unmysterious, never something one can take for granted or presume to move around, like a piece on one's chessboard, or even an x-factor in one's mappings of reality.

If so, then one cannot approach interreligious dialogue, where comparative approaches to Christ are inevitable, like a full democrat, or the sort of gentleman who would blush ever to be found putting forward claims to uniqueness. Uniqueness is at the heart of the Christian confession, even after one has agreed that claims to uniqueness understandably come forward from other religious traditions. For Christian faith there can be no higher viewpoint from which to adjudicate such various claims. The faithful believer cannot surrender Christ to the judgment of religious studies or some universal religious standpoint. Always Christ is the alpha and omega, because he is one's savior.

Christ in Indian Perspective

We mentioned that historicity is an important factor when comparing Jesus and the Buddha, and we may begin reflecting on this factor by noting the tendency of the Indian cultural matrix from which the Buddha arose to downplay history. Such downplaying has not been a matter of denying that human beings exist in space and time. It has not been a matter of denying that what happens to people in their child-hood influences their adulthood, or denying that what was happening in his village at the time a holy man began to preach had no bearing on his preaching. It has been rather a matter of thinking that truly impor-tant experiences and truths escape time, with the result that historicity —being embodied in time, being shaped by time—cannot be a prison. One can escape from history, with its truckloads of karmic bondage, by activating one's inmost selfhood. The best way to such activation is by stopping the flames of desire. Other ways include becoming ecstatic (stepping out of history) through love of a divinity and gaining an intuitive understanding, a vision, of the nothingness with which human existence is partnered and on which it depends.

The impact of this general Indian sense of history on Asians' un-derstanding of the Buddha seems to have been to downplay the signifi-cance of his time, place, individual characteristics, and other personal, idiosyncratic aspects. In principle the Buddha has been precious not for his body or his biography but for his spirit, his enlightenment.

In Indian perspective, therefore, the Christian insistence on the significance of the flesh of Jesus can seem peculiar. Surely it was the wisdom of Jesus and his union with divinity that were important, not his having come from Galilee or spoken in distinctly Jewish figures (par-ables). Why, then, have Christians made his flesh sacramental? Why have they made their central rite not simply a remembrance of his teaching, a representation of his death and resurrection, but an eating of his flesh and drinking of his blood? Doesn't such an approach to Jesus, such a Christian spirituality, canonize things which, as historical and finite, cannot possibly bear the weight of the divine? It is one thing to say that all revelations of divinity to human beings have to occur in history. It is another to refuse to pry the historical container away from the divinity revealed, to insist that, at least in the case of Jesus, those who saw him in the flesh saw his Father.

So Indian sensibilities are another route to the scandal of particu-larity and historicity that climaxes in the incarnation, with its conse-quent passion, death, and resurrection. Speaking for those impressed by the priority of spirit in human understandings of the divine, Indian thinkers have shied away from the particularity of Jesus of Nazareth, being more willing to discuss the Christ (his universal principle, as they saw it) than the one born of Mary. They have been willing to welcome Jesus as an avatar, a manifestation-form, of divinity, and to place him alongside Krishna, Rama, the Buddha, and other avatars. With the exception of those who converted to orthodox Christianity, they have not been willing to take fully seriously the Christian insistence that the one whom Mary bore was the infinite Word.

Now, one great virtue of the characteristically Indian approach to religious diversity has been to promote tolerance. Granted, Hindus, Buddhists, Sikhs, Jains, Muslims, and others who flourished on the subcontinent have had their bloody persecutions. Nonetheless, the blend of Aryan idealism and pre-Aryan polytheism that one finds at the roots of Hindu spirituality has fostered a widespread sense that truth has many valid forms. Indeed, it may have fostered the notion that truth is as much plural as singular, a notion that could not be separated from the Indian perceptiveness about the colorations of consciousness—the permutations of desire.

At any rate, it is well for Christians to take a lesson from Indian appreciations of tolerance and Indian aversion to fanaticism. What the Bhagavad-Gita canonized in laying out various paths to salvation, including the democratic path of love (bhakti), should prompt careful meditation in Christian circles. Were Christians to take the historicity of Jesus fully to heart, they could well appreciate the loss of faith entailed in promoting allegiance to Christ fanatically. As well, they could appreciate the foundations for such useful policies as letting Jews and Muslims develop their own interpretations of Jesus.

Jesus knew that the mixture of determinism and freedom in the hearts of the people he met was known only to God. As much as he felt that in rejecting his message about the kingdom of God audiences were rejecting their great chance for salvation, he left people the right to say no. From within Christian faith, it may seem inconceivable that one could hear the words of Jesus and not find them words of everlasting life, or that one could witness the cures of Jesus and not find in them the power of God. Such noncomprehension bites at the edges of the gospel of John, tempting the author to attribute the rejection of Jesus by "the Jews," John's pejorative term for Jesus' antagonists, to hardness of heart (bad will, sinfulness). But Jesus himself apparently accepted the fact that unchartable forces were at work. The Johannine notion of "faith" therefore is immeasurably rich, for it includes the very ability to hear and see the communications of God. Why some people open themselves and others close themselves is wrapped in counsels known only to God.

This view of christological faith, which one can clarify and develop from within a following of Jesus that gives the New Testament some pride of place, has immensely useful, if delicate, implications for interreligious dialogue. If they wish, Christians can consider the choices of those from other faiths with whom they are in dialogue mysterious matters beyond human ken. Those who don't possess Christian faith, and seem to have no desire to possess it, stand outside the circle, the horizon, that the spirited Christian believer comprehends. The best posture would seem to be to leave such people in the hands of God, who certainly can provide them all that they need to live well.

Where such a posture becomes delicate is in the need to credit one's own faith with no superiority. It is virtually impossible to have a robust, satisfying Christian faith and not wish that others shared it, but those whose faith is mature enough to immerse them in the obscurities of divine providence should be able to retain a proper humility about their own sense of good fortune. Moreover, they should be able to notice the many ways in which people of other faiths may outstrip them, even in qualities highly esteemed on Christian grounds. The depth, sincerity, self-sacrifice, and holiness of people not pledging allegiance to Jesus is sufficient word to the Christian wise to keep them modest about their understanding of God's ways, as well as about their own religious performance.

Such a modesty befits the Indian outlook with which we began. For Indian spirituality, there is plenty of time in which to make progress toward salvation (moksha). One need not strain and press, grow intolerant and short-tempered. The ignorance that blocks people's way to salvation may be undercut slowly by the workings of experience. For those who begin to free themselves from ignorance, something good will shape their next existence. Painful as the passage from birth to death to rebirth again is, one must make peace with its necessities. Peace is the partner of detachment, which is another name for realism.

The correlative for Christians interested in interreligious dialogue would seem to be patience with the mysteries in which they find themselves involved. If people have various kinds of faith, so be it. Such variety need not trouble those secure in their love of Christ. It need not cause them to doubt the validity of their own commitments or God's provision for those making non-Christian commitments. There is no necessary contradiction between the uniqueness of Christ and the variety of the world's paths to salvation. Christ can be sought and known under many different guises.

The Human Consciousness of Christ

Any treatment of the human consciousness (awareness) of Jesus Christ has to reckon with the limitations consequent on his having been fully a member of our species. Thus, it has to note that he did not know all languages, all sciences, all maps of the world. Moreover, he did not have unlimited stamina, perception, good fortune. If he were pricked, he would bleed. If he were insulted, he would suffer. He had to eat, sleep, eliminate, and ponder the vagaries of human behavior as all other human beings before and after him have been forced to do.

And yet, of course, Jesus was different. For Christian faith, his humanity was so united with divinity that his humanity was perfected. The major symbol of this perfected humanity has been the Christian conviction that Jesus was sinless. He did not fail his humanity the way other people of his day did. While he had to be finite, on penalty of forfeiting his status as a member of our species, he did not have to be warped, sullied, deflected from his goals the way the rest of human beings have been. Naturally, to claim that Jesus was sinless is provocative. Naturally, it stirs the sort of resentment and incredulity stirred by the other aspects of the Christian claim for his uniqueness. The basis of this Christian claim is faith about the incarnation, which developed from the effort to understand just who and what this remarkable man had been. But the claim that Jesus was sinless has been nearly as provocative as the claim that his humanity was united with divinity. Indeed, human beings probably have more experience of transcendence (movement into the divine beyond) than they have of sinlessness: moral beauty without flaw. Probably it has been easier to accredit the notion that divinity might take flesh than to accept the reality of a true human being enjoying complete moral health, never dragged down into things petty, shameful, or loveless.

Accepting the traditional Christian confession of the sinlessness of Christ, let us muse about its likely implications. Naturally, this is quite speculative, because we cannot call Jesus before us as a witness, except in the imaginative way of interrogating his New Testament portrait. Even less can we open his brain to determine whether any of its waves were unique. Still, it is instructive to speculate in this way, not only because it helps us appreciate better the consequences of saintliness, but also because it helps us appreciate the thrust of salvation—God's work to perfect our humanity.

Jesus apparently enjoyed a remarkable, unique familiarity with God. The very fact that Jesus called God his "Father," using a term (Abba) that implied familial intimacy, made him stand out from the vast majority of his contemporaries. Their first notion of God stressed the divine distance and sovereignty. Their first word for God was "Lord." Jesus never fails in respect toward his God, but he does presume intimacy and mutual understanding. Convinced that his work comes from his Father, he depends on the Father's support and power to preach, heal, teach, and resist the incursions of evil. He does not blanch when he meets opposition, and he refuses to stay silent when that would produce distortion. Without denying the legitimacy of the religious authorities of his day, he claims that such authorities have their significant limits. All of this Jesus does out of the fullness of his relationship with his Father, and in the power of the Spirit who signals the presence of divinity to and in him. The resource that Jesus finds inexhaustible is precisely his Father's love. To believe, as Jesus urges his hearers to do, is to commit oneself to the Father in a similar trust. It is to take a similarly childlike stance of knowing, without doubt, that the Father can only want good things on one's behalf and is bound to stand at one's side.

Perhaps the sinlessness of Jesus was manifested more by this unbreakable trust than by his endurance of fools, knaves, even those who eventually secured his death. The majority of us flee those who offend us or would do us harm, but we can imagine being courageous enough to withstand them. Who, though, can imagine being courageous enough, morally equipped, to withstand the scrutiny of God? Who can presume to be God's beloved child, an offspring bound to elicit more smiles than frowns? Saint Thérèse of the Child Jesus brought much of this audacity into focus for modern times by casting herself as a child to whom God was nearly bound to say yes. In canonizing her—making her a model for others' faith—Catholic Christianity affirmed the profundity of her instinct and its kinship with the faith, the human practice, of Jesus himself.

The carry-over for Jesus concerning his relations with other human beings was equally dramatic. Jesus became famous, notorious, for consorting with "sinners." He did not reserve his company for people of unimpeachable reputation, let alone for the wealthy and powerful of his day. He went among the tax collectors (despised by Jews as collaborators with the hated Romans) and whores, among the mad and the sickly, among those written off as failures and no-accounts. How did Jesus do this? Whence came the impetus? Apparently Jesus did it in virtue of the love of his Father, upon which he depended totally, and with the gentleness, the immediacy, that he found the Father's love to carry. Apparently the impetus to follow through on his perceptions of need, openness, or simply misery came from the love he found the Father showering on all creation, as the Father made the sun to shine, the rain to fall, on just and unjust alike.

The consciousness of Christ therefore was dominated by the Father and the Father's steadfast love. As a faithful Jew, Jesus would have loved the constant refrain of the Bible that the Lord is compassionate and merciful, long-suffering and abounding in steadfast love. He would have intuited that the crux of Israelite hope, through thick and thin, had always been the goodness of the Lord. Though human beings were ever inconstant, the Lord was a rock and salvation, one wholly reliable. Though no sage person put trust in princes, one could not over-trust the Lord. Certainly, the psalms and other dramatic expressions of Israelite faith were filled with pained, funny, complaining, fully human fussing about the troubles of human existence and the obscurity of God's ways. Certainly, the more Jesus felt the inevitability of his march toward Calvary the more the dark side of keeping faith with God became prominent. Yet Jesus felt, with Job (in one mistranslation), "though he slay me, yet will I trust him." Jesus knew that there was nothing more ultimate to which he could go, that his Father's love was the best tool he had for interpreting all of reality. This knowledge, which of course was also a commitment, an act of trust taking him beyond what he could prove on empirical grounds, colored all of his human awareness. He could not see a fig tree, or a tax collector up in a sycamore tree, or fields ripe for the harvest, or a man born blind, or a woman seeking water at the well, or his mother standing beside his cross without being moved by the Father's love. Even when that love echoed in hollows of pain, disappointment, wonder how God could ever bring goodness out of such evil, the love presumably prevailed. That is the sense of the Christian confession of Jesus' sinlessness, and that is the inference one is likely to make, when one ponders the implications of hypostatic union with the Word of divinity.

Set such a christology as a seal upon your interreligious dialogues and they may be considerably different from what they would have been. On the one hand, you will have been more forthcoming about the riches Christian faith finds in the human experience of Jesus. On the other hand, you will have heightened the need to estimate the impact that specific historical faith, with its limitations on universal availability and acceptability, can make on easy ecumenical sharing. Certainly this same faith offers powerful reasons for continuing the dialogue. Certainly the last thing that the love of God impelled in Christ was a will to power or dominance. The Son of Man, as Jesus apparently called himself, came to serve, not to lord it over others. Nonetheless, the configuration of reality that Christian spirituality finds most precious is based on a parental love that needs to be appreciated in all its awesome effectiveness in the specific historical life and personality of Jesus Christ. Not to linger with this specificity, not to appreciate why one cannot simply assimilate it to religious devotion the world over, is bound to seem an ecumenical disaster, if one is a great lover of Jesus and his Father.

The Impact of Feminism

When analysts study the effects of the traditional Christian understanding of Jesus and the incarnation, they can come upon abuses that may not have been inevitable but in fact were highly significant historically. One such abuse is making Jesus the basis for considering women second-class citizens, less than equal sharers of humanity, or of Christian faith, with men. In the words of some feminist thinkers, if God became a male, then the male became god. Even after one has entered several qualifications and distinctions, something potent remains. How is one to estimate the significance of the masculinity of Jesus, granted the contributions of Christian culture to the oppression of women?

While it is debatable that Jesus himself oppressed women, and unclear whether he wished women to have official authority in his community, it is beyond debate that women have suffered in biblical, Christian cultures because men, males, considered themselves, and were considered by many women, to have special rights to power. Even when one points out the important facts that power in the community of Jesus was supposed to be mainly ministerial, and that closeness to Jesus was always a matter of love rather than office, the fact remains that many women failed to flourish as they might have, or were actually abused, because of the dominant Christian conception that males were more the images of God than females. Whether they should have or not, many Christian leaders, including otherwise admirable theologians and saints, buttressed this male primacy by appealing to the truth of faith that it was in the male Jesus of Nazareth that the Logos found its human expression. The fact that the flesh of Jesus came from Mary may have mitigated any strictly theological inferences about the primacy of male flesh, but in ordinary cultural parlance the masculinity of Jesus told women that even God expected them to hear and obey. Otherwise, why would the divine have made a male voice its primary oracle?

The history of women's experiences within Christianity, including the history of their encounters with Jesus in often fulfilling prayer, suggests that the feminist implications of christology are immensely complicated. We can never get close to the full actuality of "history," and the value-judgments that we make from our present vantage points can run counter to the value-judgments made by the people we are studying. Nonetheless, today's feminists, male as well as female, are correct to recognize that any discussion of the unique value of the person and teaching of Jesus is liable to draw demurs from some articulate women. In fact the impetus to the new witchcraft attractive to many feminists is often a desire to escape from the sexism of Christian tradition. The more knowledgeable parties to such an escape may recognize that Jesus is less the culprit than those who followed him in leading the Christian community, but the common membership of the covens is likely to account Jesus an enemy, or the representative of an oppressive phase of history now thankfully not necessary.

Instructively, Jesus is not unique in receiving blame for historical abuses of which he may be quite innocent. It is hard to know precisely what the social conditions were in the Buddha's day, or in Muhammad's day, and precisely what the Buddha or Muhammad desired for women. The same holds for Jesus. Still, it seems clear that in all three cases the culture contemporary to the great founder was patriarchal, in the sense that it assumed male rule. Such "rule" was multi-dimensional, touching religion and home life as well as politics. As lived out, patriarchal cultures tended to generate many exceptions and counter-weights to male rule. Women having little official power or status sometimes could acquire considerable clout simply by virtue of their talent, or powerful personalities, or religious gifts. At any rate, the message of any great innovator on the one hand assumed a prevailing culture, usually patriarchal, and on the other hand sought to transform that culture. When we contemplate the transformations of sexual relations explicit or implicit in the messages of great founders such as Jesus, Muhammad, and the Buddha, we start to appreciate the depth and complexity of the symbols mediating sexual relations (in any culture).

Femaleness and maleness constitute what is arguably the most basic difference in human affairs. Granted, some theorists argue that class or race is equally primordial, yet sex has a certain biological priority that gives it powerful claims. As well, sex clearly has psychological and cultural dimensions that multiply its significance, as well as a regular desire to overcome differences that makes it suggestive politically. For the sexual majority, which is heterosexual, this regular desire takes biological, psychological, and cultural form. It is so significant for personal fulfillment, in the mode of romantic love, and so crucial to procreation, that many would call it the most powerful force in human history. For the sexual minority, which is homosexual, the desire for union is scarcely less significant, regularly appearing as powerful in the lives of same-sex lovers as in the lives of heterosexuals.

The best approach to the implications of feminist reappraisals of Jesus might be to concentrate on what sort of love faith in Jesus enables and what sort it discourages. If Jesus in fact urged his followers to a passionate love of the divine mystery (his Father) that freed them from many bonds, then much of the repression associated with Christian love may appear to be illegitimate. Granted absorption with the Father like that of Jesus, what should have become of sexual relations among Christians, and what should women have experienced? These are not easy questions, to be sure, if only because the New Testament itself seems to present both egalitarian and patriarchal strata. As well, one has to decide what the freedom consequent on the love of Jesus should have allowed era by era.

In fact, one of the findings of feminist probes of the behavior of Jesus suggests that for him personally the love of God led to freer relationships with women than what the typical rabbi of his day enjoyed. We have mentioned his associating with tax collectors and whores. We could also mention his willingness to deal with Samaritan women, his friendship with Martha and Mary, the special attachments he allowed Mary Magdalene. All of these are filtered through layers of New Testament tradition that may slant them significantly from what the historical man Jesus of Nazareth actually said and did. But they are our only sources, and it is encouraging that they show a figure willing and able to enter into the mutuality of concern characteristic of mature friendship between men and women.

The question of erotic love, in the sense of the desire for heterosexual intercourse, stands outside the parameters of traditional Christian devotion toward Jesus, inasmuch as the regular teaching handed down made Jesus a celibate for the sake of serving the kingdom of his Father. The question of friendship therefore is simpler, and perhaps equally instructive. Jesus allowed women to be disciples, most notably so in sending Magdalene to announce the resurrection. He treated Martha and Mary warmly, and many of his cures went to heal women. Women showed him some of the examples of faith that touched him most deeply, and they gave of their financial substance to support his ministry and that of the early church. At the least, then, the love emanating from Jesus included women, inviting them into the embrace of divine friendship.

Equally, the love emanating from Jesus removed women from the status of disrespect that patriarchal cultures regularly have foisted upon them. Neither the bodies of women, nor their personality traits, nor their social roles alienated them from Jesus. If anything, Jesus warmed to women in a special way because women frequently showed him special faith. Perhaps because they had greater need, or were willing and able to show their need, women tended to reach out to Jesus, welcome his message, and ask his help. So the crux of discipleship—being a believer—fitted the women of Jesus' day very well. Little indicates that women of subsequent eras were less apt for faith and discipleship. In principle, therefore, Christianity undercut the disadvantages women suffered in much patriarchal culture, spotlighting the values that Jesus prized—openness, fidelity, love, sacrifice—and suggesting strongly that women were at least the equals of men in exhibiting these values. When Christian eras showed themselves sexist, they contradicted judgments of their master. The question then became how to keep the baby and throw out the bathwater. Usually the reforms necessary to make women full partners in official Christian culture were more radical than what male power-bearers would allow, but the men's refusal only put them in conflict with Jesus, despite all their rationalization and hiding behind their offices. For Christian feminists, the tragi-comic result now is having to expose the un-Christian character of the powers who oppose justice and love toward the women who constitute the majority of the church's membership. Ideally, the support of the Holy Spirit, encountered in deep prayer, tips the scales to the side of comedy, so that laughter and hope prevail over tears and depression.[5]

Feminism, Social Justice, and Christology

Inasmuch as the agenda of feminists targets full equality between the sexes, feminism becomes a species of work for social justice. Across the board, social justice can appeal to the profound human instinct, cultivated by the Bible, that God requires fair-dealing. Such fair-dealing, we now see, applies always and everywhere: in racial relations, economics, international affairs, dealings between labor and management, interactions between churches and states. Neither the young nor the old have a monopoly on rights or responsibilities. Both natives and newcomers have something to give and something to receive. When the Israelite prophets spoke of dealing correctly, mercifully, with the widow and the orphan before turning to sacrifice to God, they underscored the ties between love of neighbor and love of God. The first fulfillment of the commandment to love neighbor as self is to render neighbor justice. Those who come before God with dirty hands in this regard should not expect an easy hearing.

It makes sense, therefore, to place christological issues alongside issues of social justice and ask what impact the view of Jesus developed by Christian love should have on fair-dealing. In the context of interreligious dialogue, it makes sense to ask how Christian treatment of non-Christians has been warped by christological convictions, illegitimate or legitimate. The strange thing is the problematic character many partners to interreligious dialogue attribute to christology. To their mind, confessing a great love for Jesus can be less a boon to social justice than a bane or burden. Let us examine this reaction.

On the occasion of a visit to Tulsa for a celebration of the twenty-fifth anniversary of the Vatican II "Decree on Religious Liberty," Rabbi Leon Klenicki delivered himself of some impromptu criticisms of liberation theology. When challenged, he pointed to the unsophisticated exegesis found among some early exponents of Latin American liberation theology, which contrasted the old and new covenants more starkly, and more to the advantage of Christianity, than has become usual or approved in circles of either biblical scholarship or ecumenical dialogue. But what about the magnificent defense that Latin American liberation theology was making of the rights of the poor, the illiterate, the sick, the politically marginalized, even the murdered in Latin America? How fair, or commonsensical, was it to attack such an heroic expression of biblical faith and concern for justice because it lagged behind in areas such as sensitivity to the religious rights of Jews (or the wholesale rights of women, or environmental problems)? Was it not likely that the Latin American liberation theologians, if put on notice that they were giving offense on these matters or had miles to go, could agree and make reforms easily, because their own principles held them to justice everywhere? But they were not going to get such slack and good will from Rabbi Klenicki, any more than they were going to get it from certain militant feminists. As in the case of many people concerned with the question of abortion, one issue had to take center stage. Naturally, one can charge the Latin American liberation theologians with having had blinders also, and for all groups—liberation theologians, anti-abortionists, pro-abortionists, Jews recalling the holocaust —history provides many exculpations. But if one wants to be frank and thorough, the fact is that any limitation on our sympathy for people spending themselves to achieve social justice deserves divinity. Certainly we have to discuss mutual oversights, the problems we are causing one another, and the baggage of history. But we also have to generate good will, have the political acumen to recognize allies, and keep some sense of the big picture, the full outreach of God's justice. We also have to praise those willing to spend their lives helping the poor and the oppressed, regularly counting them our betters in the service of God.

To turn to the bottom line, is it unjust and a detriment to ecumenical relations to confess the divinity of Jesus Christ and grant him a privileged place in one's faith? Does such a confession inevitably lead to anti-semitism, sexism, an inability to participate humbly, democratically, in civic affairs, ecumenical discussions, coalitions concerned with national or international problems? No, of course not. De facto, many people making such a traditional Christian commitment have shown themselves to be good friends to Jews, to women, to ecumenical relations, to civil rights, to work for justice on a dozen different fronts. De jure, any theologian aware of the distinction between the status of Jesus and the status of Jesus' follower has the key to the puzzle Christians must solve. To say that Jesus is nonpareil is not to say that the follower of Jesus has special rights in civil or ecumenical matters, any more than to say that Muhammad is nonpareil (for Muslims) is to say that Muslims have special rights in civil or ecumenical matters. The same holds for Jews, Buddhists, Hindus, other religionists, and non-religionists. Granted, it took centuries for this simple distinction to evolve, and the American experiment in pluralism (having no established religion) still has not won the hearts of many traditional religionists, most Muslims and some Roman Catholics prominent among them. But in itself the confession of the unique character of the center of one's life is not undemocratic or bound to cause bias. In itself the confession of the unique character of the center of one's life is simply an act of honesty and health. So, there is nothing objectionable in the New Testament's presentation of Jesus as the messiah, with the consequent implication that a new era of salvation history has begun, any more than there is anything objectionable in the Muslim presentation of Muhammad as the seal of the prophets, the one consummating the line of Abraham, Moses, and Jesus. The objections rightly begin when such a presentation becomes the basis for disparaging other people and denying them civil or religious rights. That has happened, sometimes egregiously, which makes the worries of Jewish, Christian, Muslim, and other minorities understandable. But it does not make the ideal the bracketing of any ultimate allegiance, confession, or claim that given people find the world most beautiful when they view it from faith in a given teacher or savior. Such a move would enshrine agnosticism, or the truncation of the human drive to worship in specific forms, as the ideal—the "religious" option. As noted before, there is no neutral ground, when it comes to ultimate, religious matters. The interpretational horizon one takes shows one's religious commitment, when the chips are down and the issue is what one lives by.

Christology, then, labors under no special hardships when it comes to social justice. Christians have as much right to make Jesus the configuring center of their sense of the world as those who adhere to other senses of the world have the right to praise their configuring centers. Equally, Christians have as much responsibility not to impose their views and behavioral patterns on others as others have the responsibility to let Christians be. Questions remain, of course, about how to correlate public policies in countries where people do not agree. Pluralistic democracies have a tough row to hoe. The American tradition has been to protect individual liberties as much as possible, except for situations where death or great damage to the common good would result. Times of crisis put pressure on this tradition, as we now see regarding drugs, communicable diseases such as AIDS, guns, the development of wilderness areas, abortion, and other divisive issues. None of these, however, need obscure a citizen's Christian, Jewish, secular, or other ultimate allegiance. Each can be cast so as to minimize offenses to both legitimate individual rights and the religious conscience of majorities or pluralities. It may be wise or unwise to move militarily against Latin American drug lords, to institute the death penalty for drug pushers, to ban all private possession of guns, to require testing for AIDS, or to close thousands of square miles of coastal and interior lands to development permanently. Christological commitment certainly should color any Christian's view of any such matter, but it will not determine it. Abortion is a harder case, because of the closer connection between the defense of innocent life and the ethics of Jesus, but even with abortion Christians cannot be simpleminded. In fact, deep christological commitment, as, no doubt, deep Muslim commitment to the Qur'an or deep Jewish commitment to the torah, makes healthy believers the enemies of simplemindedness. Aware of the mysteriousness of all human ventures under God, they feel great pressure to be tolerant. Indeed, if you find yourself facing a fanatic, you can be sure you're not facing a profoundly religious person.

Christ in Buddhist Perspective

In the detachment promoted by the Buddha's concern to stifle desire and so extinguish suffering, one sees Jesus as the antagonist of fanaticism. Passionate as he was for the advent of the kingdom of God, for the glory of his Father, he never compelled faith in God or personal allegiance to himself. As interpreted by the evangelists, he did warn people of the dire consequences of refusing the overtures of God. He did speak of hellfire and brimstone. Yet this was not his prevailing speech, and, as the evangelists present the matter, he was provoked by the religious authorities of his time, who were unable to give him a fair hearing, because of their concern to maintain their own position.

The Buddha is notoriously cool to Christian sensibility, so one can question whether this dispassionate view of Jesus is accurate. Jesus, after all, was not a child of India. He derived from the passionate line of the prophets: Isaiah, Jeremiah, Ezekiel. On the other hand, Jesus seems a sapiential figure, as well as a prophet, and dispassion, in the sense of letting what unfolds stay in the hands of God, is the great mark of the sapiential figure. Well aware of his human limitations, the sage realizes that only God can write straight with the crooked lines of history. Only God can deliver justice, salvation, divinization—the great treasures on which the human heart is set.

But the Buddhist seems to demur. Salvation, the Buddha seems to say, is a human affair, something that men and women can realize for themselves. Let them sink into the Four Noble Truths, realize the pith and frame of suffering, get such realization into their marrow and soul-stuff, and they will see in a liberating flash. The fetters of karma and ignorance will fall away. They will know, beyond words or doubts, that there is nothing to desire, no self to do the desiring. They will accept the fact that, for the enlightened, things already are full of light and quite perfect. No gods or other external agents have to effect this salvation. Human beings will be made whole, carried back from their alienation, ushered into the health they always sensed was their great potential, by their own efforts. Just as Gautama gained enlightenment, liberation, by vowing not to move from the pipal tree, so the follower of Gautama who musters equal resolve is sure to succeed.

But suppose the alienation is not simply within the human being, or between human beings, or even between the human being and the cosmos. Suppose the alienation, the ignorance and desire causing the suffering, is between the creature and its creator. Does it follow that the creator has to be party to the process of liberation, has to effect the salvation of the creature as an act of grace? Buddhism does not speak of a creator, a personal force bringing the material world into being from nothingness, so the question does not fit Buddhist categories. Christians, however, are forced to configure the question of salvation in these terms, because Christians follow the diction of Jesus, whose world took shape from the creative love of his all-providing Father.

The dispassion in which Jesus traded was an indifference to both his own fate and the judgments of other people. Compared to pleasing his Father, doing his Father's will, Jesus accounted his rejection, his defeat, even his death quite secondary. This did not make him masochistic, but it did give his life a stark clarity that remains shocking twenty centuries later. There was something much more important to Jesus than his own life, let alone his own success. There was a relationship, a love, that set him free of the fears and ambitions constraining most of his contemporaries, indeed constraining most human beings who have dotted the earth. So Jesus could be dispassionate about the Pharisees, the crowds who refused his message, even the disciple who betrayed him. He warmed to their challenge and he felt their rejection, but never so as to put in jeopardy either his trust in his Father or the joy that serving his Father brought. Buddhists might say that the love Jesus lavished on his Father limited his detachment and impeded his enlightenment. They might say that to pray in petition, or even in praise, is to manifest a mind still unconverted to right thoughts and the other constituents of the Noble Eightfold Path. Christians have to say that at this point the two systems seem incomparable, for Christians cannot conceive of anything more basic, vivifying, or saving than the love of the Father, the Spirit, animating Jesus.

How does the risen Christ now regard Buddhists, or Jews, or Muslims—people offering interpretations of him different from the interpretations that his followers find in the New Testament and consider canonical? This is a highly speculative question, of course, but it makes sense to answer, "highly." Not only do the New Testament authors and Christian tradition, for all their canonicity, never exhaust the possible meanings of the love binding Jesus to the Father and the Spirit. There is also good reason to think that Buddhist, Muslim, Jewish, and other convictions in fact have helped many people answer the equivalents of the questions that Jesus was posing to his followers.

Jesus was asking his followers to trust that God, the great mystery of their lives, had good things in store for them. He was asking his followers to trust that love would open to them a world of wonders— beauty and truth sufficient to let them triumph over evil and death. The Buddha, Muhammad, Moses, and many other great religious leaders were asking similar things of their followers: take the Four Noble Truths to heart, submit yourselves wholly to Allah, believe in the covenant and follow its torah. Do these things, all these teachers were saying, and you will find the path to liberation, to pleasing Allah on judgment day, to life.

The message was a call to faith. The message was an invitation to escape present burdens and fetters, to open oneself to new horizons and powers. For those with the depth to appreciate it, the message was a call to conversion, new beginnings, a sea-change. Jesus spoke with the conviction of one seared unto bliss by an unearthly love. The Buddha spoke with the serenity of one who had passed outside the clutches of karma and desire. Muhammad spoke as the friend of God, the perfect submitter who had been made God's mouthpiece. Moses spoke with the awe of one who had seen the hind parts of God and been preserved from incineration. There is no need for Christians to disparage the speech of such other religious heroes. There is no need for Christians to initiate comparisons among the four visions or teachings for the purpose of ranking them. Christians are bound to consider the message and person of Jesus completely sufficient for salvation: the healing of broken human existence and conveyance of human beings into beatifying intimacy with God. They are not bound to claim that Jesus exhausted the ways of being the revelation or the wisdom or the salvation of God.

Christ and Liberation

The way to deny the uniqueness of Christ among humanity's resources for liberation is to show that other great teachers demonstrated how to free human beings from their worst chains. The way to affirm the uniqueness of Christ among humanity's resources for liberation is to argue that all such paths to freedom depend for their efficacy on the love of God that Christ incarnated singularly. Both ways can claim evidence, logic, and persuasiveness. The differences between them boil down to the differences between making one's estimates on the basis of a detached comparison among the great religious teachers and making one's estimates on the basis of the wholehearted commitment to Christ called faith.

Two questions immediately come to mind. First, does wholehearted commitment to Christ in faith in fact necessitate finding his incarnation of divine love singular? Second, is wholehearted commitment to Christ in faith rational, responsible, something that an adult citizen of today's global culture can do in good conscience?

On the first question, opinions perhaps will vary. In our view, however, the line of evaluation indicated by Peter's "To whom shall we go? You have the words of eternal life" makes Jesus singular, unique, nonpareil, unsurpassable. This line of evaluation flowered in the Johannine theology that made Jesus the incarnation of the Logos. One could not go beyond the union with divinity accomplished in the flesh of Christ, because that union was hypostatic: so perfect that the Logos was Jesus (provided the foundations of Jesus' "I"). When the Johannine Christ says, "I am," echoing the speech of the biblical Lord, the author of John holds nothing back. He depicts those opposing Jesus as understanding that Jesus is equating himself with God, his Father. Before Abraham came to be, Jesus was, because what Jesus now is coheres in the Word that was with God from the beginning, the Word in which all things were made. One can ask whether this Johannine language is faithful to how the historical Jesus spoke and thought, but one cannot answer negatively without either overstepping the bounds of what we know about the historical Jesus or calling into question the reliability of the canonical New Testament as a whole. For Christians, the canonical New Testament is an imperfect, limited set of documents, but there is nothing better, nothing more basic behind it to which one can go for correction or arbitration. Even though the New Testament depended on the living faith of the Christian community in its arising, and has depended on that faith down the ages for its interpretation, there is nothing in the Christian repertoire that has a higher authority. If one rejects the Johannine, or the Pauline, or the Markan, or any other canonical interpretation of Jesus, one cuts oneself off from the most privileged access to Christ that Christians have treasured for nineteen hundred years.

We have stressed the Johannine view of the incarnation, but we could also approach the singularity of Jesus through the Pauline view of redemption, or the synoptics' views of what Jesus revealed, how he healed human beings, what he meant for the history of Israel, how he extended salvation to all humankind. One would have to do cartwheels, or simply distort what the New Testament documents (or the conciliar documents) say, to come up with a Jesus who is not singular, unique, the decisive happening in history, the end-event opening to human beings the kingdom of God. Therefore, if one wants to join the cloud of witnesses who have committed themselves to Jesus through the ages, one has to make the liberation that Jesus accomplished, secured and made available, one of a kind.

Granted that, is it necessary to profess such a view of Jesus to be a Christian? Can one not call oneself a Christian because, even though one is not prepared to make such weighty (divine) claims for Jesus, one finds Jesus admirable, the best teacher or leader around whom to rally? Once again, opinions will vary, and certainly the history of Christianity is filled with people who have professed allegiance to Jesus but not accepted the high christology we have outlined. In our opinion, however, the full weight of Christian faith, and the full benefits, only swing into action when one takes the original witness to Jesus on its own terms and accepts Jesus as the personal event that changed human existence. Further, we distinguish between the core of the original witness, which we place in such eschatology (definitiveness), and less ultimate matters such as Jesus' miracles or the particular theories of Paul. Jesus' miracles were an integral part of what his early followers perceived him to be, but it is impossible for us, today, to know exactly what they entailed. The particular theories of Paul about Jesus' relation to Adam or the necessity of Jesus' cross are woven into the matrix of early Christian faith, but it is arguable that other views of the eschatological significance of what happened in Jesus merit equal consideration. The one thing that remains, after one has sifted through the different strata and visions of the New Testament sources, is their common testimony to the definitive character of what happened in Jesus Christ. In the light of Christ's resurrection, the world turned over, human existence was redone (or newly presented), a light now shone that was stronger than the darkness of human fear, ignorance, malice, and even death. In the flesh of Jesus, what eye had not seen, ear had not heard, it had not entered the human heart to conceive had been brought within human reach, made amenable to human touch. The love of God, come into human flesh, had gained voice, gesture, a way to suffer human outrage and rejection directly. It had also gained a way to triumph over all such outrage and rejection, all the fear and darkness in the human heart, and resurrect the human project, taking it so far beyond the grave that it entered eternal life (another great Johannine symbol). One who holds back from this center of the Christian confession ends up with terribly thin gruel. A good news that does not take humanity out of its terrible darkness, into ineffable light and life, is so much less than what the early Christians experienced that it scarcely deserves mention in the same breath.

Second, however, is such wholehearted commitment to Christ in faith rational, responsible, something that an adult citizen of today's global culture can make in good conscience? Why not? Because many other religious pathways claim to be redemptive, revelatory, divinizing? Because history is full of religious frauds? Because nothing that has appeared in history is unlimited, and being unlimited, unconditioned, is the necessary condition of being worthy of wholehearted allegiance? Because the Buddha or the Qur'an or the torah or the Tao might approximate, or equal, or better what Christians confess they find in Jesus?

Each of these grounds for denying the rationality of Christian commitment is a species of the historicism mentioned earlier, and each founders just as historicism does. If you refuse to choose, you have in fact chosen. If you say one can never know, you have in fact claimed to know. The question is not whether you are going to choose. The question is what you are going to choose to live by, to give your life coherence, to furnish you the hope, the spiritual succor, on which creativity, usefulness to others, and peace of soul depend. Granted the immense treasuries of peace and joy, succor and grace, that Christian faith has furnished human beings down the ages, it seems ludicrous to say that a timid agnosticism is obviously preferable. Despite all the difficulties that Christians' abuses of faith and power raise up, a thousand such difficulties do not constitute a doubt requiring agnosticism. The thrust of such doubt is to the heart of the human being and matter. There one either says yes or no, I will go on or I will refuse. And there the allure of Jesus, the appeal of Jesus, stands forth in all its naked beauty: God so loved the world; even when our hearts condemn us, God can liberate us, and God's liberation is beautiful.

The Temper of the Pluralist

Tom Driver, writing an elegant conclusion to a collection of essays to which we have referred several times, expresses his personal love for pluralism, making this personal love the energy of an argument against a unique or exclusive Jesus.[6] It is a winning confession, and an interesting argument. Let us muse about its drifts and implications.

Variety is a striking, fascinating, often beautiful feature of both the natural and human worlds. One can walk along a lonely beach and think that its beauty must be unique, cannot have an equal anywhere else. The next year one can stand high in the mountains, or in the desert, or in a field of grasses moved by the spring wind and feel much the same. The lesson, it seems, is that we should never judge that a place is singularly beautiful. Until we have exhausted all the places on earth, which of course we never shall, we should keep a modest reserve about our exclamations and judgments.

The semanticist will demand that we attend to the ambiguities in the word "singularly" before passing on to theological inferences. "Singularly" might mean of a class unto itself, with or without overtones of supremacy. A place can be the most beautiful conjunction of sea, land, and sky in one precise constellation without implying that it is more beautiful than another constellation of sea, land, and sky two hundred miles down the coast, to say nothing of constellations of land and sky in the mountains or the desert or the plains.

On one level, then, there is no problem, even for the pluralist, in saying that Christ was a unique incarnation of divine love. Every incarnation of divine love—that of other religious founders and that of Christian saints—has been unique. Does this mean, however, that Christians have to limit their claims for the significance of Christ, in the sense of not claiming that what happened in Jesus never happened anywhere else or had a significance, for all human beings, that no other personal event ever did? Do Christians have to surrender their evaluative sense of singularity, uniqueness, significance, according to which Jesus had the words of eternal life and nowhere else could one find such words in such measure and efficacy?

The reasons for saying yes are that saviors have been several, grace has abounded in many ways, human beings have trodden numerous paths to sainthood and wisdom. Empirically, then, one is foolhardy to speak of uniqueness or claim special efficacy. The pluralist is an empiricist, most moved by the profusion of species, the alternations of patterns, the seemingly endless stream of new people, new ideas, new beauties. So the pluralist takes to heart the new knowledge of humanity's religious diversity, the new appreciation of religious creativity that the past century of scholarship has brought forward, and is embarrassed by the notion of claiming for Jesus something singular, of another order, unsurpassable. That seems unwarranted in view of the cornucopia of religious achievements, and rather provincial. In ecumenical situations, it can seem gauche, a matter of bad taste.

From the inside of Christian faith, however, there are many reasons for saying that Christians do not have to surrender their sense that Jesus is singular, without compare, an achievement beyond which humanity has never gone and in principle could never go. We have indicated some of these reasons: loving personal experience of Jesus, the Johannine and other early theological interpretations of Jesus, the liturgical tradition of the Christian community (founded in its experiences of worshiping God through wholehearted faith in Jesus). At this juncture, however, it may be well to note that, for those standing within the circle of faith, there is no good reason to prefer the variety that charms the pluralist, or the embarrassment that can overtake the ecumenist, to what they have experienced with Christ. Indeed, the authority of such a variety seems completely unequal to the authority of the key religious experiences warranting the Christian's confession that Jesus is Savior and Lord. One experience is conveying a sense of creativity, richness, open horizons. The other experience is conveying a sense of healing, unique fulfillment, divinization. The realities named in the second sequence seem incomparably more profound than the realities named in the first sequence.

The pluralist could put forward the argument that the creativity, richness, open horizons that his or her peak experience brings convey something truly religious, something worthily called divine. The ordinary pluralist or empiricist seldom makes this argument, but it may lodge in many pluralists' hearts. The conclusion to such an argument could be that pluralism is a religious option preferable to opting for Jesus as the definitive, privileged revelation and conveyance of divinity. By embracing many different saviors and sages, one might be honoring God better than by embracing only Christ. Some distinctions are necessary (one can embrace Christ wholeheartedly and still admire other religious figures, in effect embracing them partially; it may not be possible to embrace many different saviors, whether collectively or serially), but for our purposes the contrast can stand.

Refuting the claim that pluralism honors God better than a prefer-

ential option for Christ involves one in judgments and choices ultimately inseparable from one's existential position in the world. There is
no way to make a detached, academic judgment about a matter going so
directly to the heart of the human project, the human need to find/
create a path through the wilderness. From within traditional Christian
faith, however, the idea of growing out of a wholehearted commitment
to Jesus and subsuming one's admiration for him under a wider-ranging
admiration of a variety of religious heroes sets off alarms. For it suggests
that the wonders of Christ could be exhausted, whereas the Christian
mystics speak regularly of the inexhaustible riches of Christ. It suggests
the being ashamed of Christ, the disowning of Christ, of which Jesus
himself warned (Mk 8:38; Lk 9:26). And it suggests a concern with
novelty, the latest fad, that makes faith superficial. All of these are
strong charges, but it would not be hard to find backing for them in
either the New Testament or the counsels of the most revered Christian
spiritual guides.

Perhaps the special pathos hanging over this discussion, however,
is the degree to which it seems unnecessary. If one has come to love the
Johannine Christ, the sacramental flesh brimming with divine life,
light, and love, one easily sees it present in myriad places, myriad cultural forms. It is not alien to Buddhism, and Buddhism is not alien to it.
It is not alien to Judaism, Islam, Hinduism, or admirable secularism.
Each of these different vestments naturally calls for further discussion,
mutual critique between Christian observer and non-Christian ob-
served. But the Christian wanting a Catholic spirituality can almost
always find a way to feel at home. The treasuries of Christian religious
experience are such that virtually always there will be an analogue, a
place to start, a bridge half built. And the literal infinity of the Logos
enfleshed assures that even when the analogue is not apparent the
sympathy and search for congeniality have good grounds.

The Catholic Christian sense of Christ is that in him humanity
was perfected, so that nothing human need be foreign to Christian
faith. This dovetails with a conviction that faith perfects human nature,
so that whenever human nature realizes a significant potential, it brings
into play the engagement with divinity, the intercourse with divinity in
love, that we imply by "faith." Whether or not one should call good
Buddhists anonymous Christians is more a matter of prudence than of
theological propriety. From within the Christian camp, in terms of

what Christians say to themselves when they ponder the riches of humanity and faith outside their institutional and cultural borders, it is completely clear that Christ can be discerned at work in the lives of Buddhists, and that Buddhists are doing anonymously, unawares, much that Christians are struggling to do knowingly, with explicit reliance on traditions passed down from Jesus.[7]

Summary Reflections I: Relativity, Transcendence, and Prayer

The humanity of Jesus Christ makes his incarnation of divine love and truth relative. There were aspects of divinity that Jesus could not incarnate, because he was limited to a given time, space, culture, language, personality. Thus one has to say that his perfect, unsurpassable incarnation of divine love and truth is perfect relative to what a human medium can accomplish and be. From the limitation intrinsic to humanity comes the space for other incarnations, salvations, personal conveyances of wisdom. Certainly the orthodox Christian will put quotation marks around the use of "incarnation" and "salvation" in such other cases. Certainly the Buddha or Muhammad will not stand on the same level as Christ. But there is no problem in admitting that God fashioned a creation and human species such that diverse ways of being moved by divine grace were virtually certain to result. As soon as one couples the thesis that God desires to communicate divine love to all human beings with the thesis that Jesus Christ was fully human, one arrives at the conclusion that from some points of view the Christian axis of salvation is bound to seem partial, limited, relative.

On the other hand, the divinity of Christ opens further horizons. If one accepts the hypostatic union of Jesus with the divine Son, a transcendent quality attaches to all of Jesus' words, actions, and effects. Each goes beyond the limitations of a simply human entity, because each conveys the limitless self-expression of the Father. As a result, each can apply always and everywhere, in a way that the words, actions, and effects of a figure not hypostatically united to the Logos cannot. One can never fix the significance or contours of such transcendence tidily, because one can never comprehend the Logos, or any other personal presence of true deity. But one can say, in the negative way appropriate to dealings with divinity that stress its infinity, that what God accomplished in and through Jesus has no equal. If, as Christian faith confesses, the Word became flesh in Christ, the memories that Christ left are mysteries in the strictest sense: deposits of meaning far richer than anything human imagination or reason or love will ever exhaust.

Two consequences for Christian prayer leap to mind. The first is that when contemplating the biblical scenes in which Jesus teaches, or heals, or suffers, or is glorified, believers do well to treat them sacramentally. Certainly it is legitimate to study them as scholars do, focusing on the literary or historical or theological goals that the writers seem to have had in mind. But they only come alive and serve Christian worship when they become pregnant with the divine Spirit. Then they bear into the present the grace, the divine life, that Jesus bore into the midst of his contemporaries. Then they become the "signs" so important in the gospel of John: ways that God showed what the divine love is like in human terms, ways that God loved the world back to health. In meeting the Jesus so pregnant with divine life, the believer finds prayer transforming. Old horizons fall away. Jesus sets new horizons.

These new horizons display possibilities not available apart from faith: divine life, immortality, forgiveness of sins, resurrection, friendship with Jesus, love of enemies, peace and joy surpassing the world's understanding. They make it credible that those who eat the flesh of the Son of Man and drink his blood abide in him as members of his body, branches of his vine, and so thrive as long as he does, and so exist with him in heaven, with the Father, among the multitudes of saints ceaselessly praising his name. All of this is nonsense to the unbeliever— pious blather. To the believer regularly contemplating the sacramental Christ, it is the most beautiful future imaginable. Although it always remains a shock, something to take one's breath away, gradually it seems fitting. This is the sort of future a God as good as the Father of Jesus would hold out. This is the sort of consummation the human heart would find, were the Father of Jesus guiding history. It is utopian, in the sense of found nowhere on earth. But it fits so perfectly with human need and human desire that often it seems more real than anything on earth ever could be.

The second consequence for Christian prayer can be a relaxed appreciation of other religious figures. One can admire the serenity of the Buddha, or Muhammad's passion for God, or the poetic sensitivity to the divine mystery available in the Lao Tzu. One can take pleasure in the stories of the boy Krishna, remarking how they humanize the divine love. One can think profitably about the images of Shiva, the Lord of the Dance of time. The Great Goddesses can pass before one's mind's eye, displaying the grace, power, and fertility of the divine mystery. One can contemplate the explosions of stellar energy, correlating them with Dante's Love that moves the stars.

These alternate images of divine being, action, or power need not challenge one's central focus on Christ. There is no necessary competition. Inasmuch as one has found Jesus to be the face of a limitless divine love, one can imagine something Christian at the marrow of everything presenting a divinity compatible with the Father of Christ. Jesus, his Father, and their Spirit remain the structure of one's religious outlook. For that to cease would be for one to surrender one's Christian allegiance. Yet one's first instinct can be not to press exclusivity but to interpret Christ inclusively, as an energy at work in all people's hearts. What people call themselves matters less than what people do. If people pursue the truth and try to love, they manifest the signs of the Spirit of Christ. If they say yes to their basic condition, trying to love the dark mystery at its depths, trying to be compassionate toward their fellow human beings, they are fighting the good fight of faith, grace, salvation.

Do Christians have to say that all people of good will, fighting such a good fight, are moved by the grace of Christ? Yes. Does this mean disparaging the Buddhist, Jewish, Hindu, secular, or other allegiances that people themselves reckon their primary resource for persevering? No, not at all. Christians can, should, say that the One God has used many different cultural traditions and forms. They can, should, say that the grace of Christ has been poured out for all people, and that wherever humanity is flourishing in truth and love, the grace of Christ is triumphing. Indeed, Christians can and should even say that wherever humanity is languishing, wherever human beings are suffering unjustly in either body or spirit, the grace of the crucified Christ is helping them bear up, is keeping humanity from complete annihilation. Nothing in the Christian conviction that grace is universal in virtue of Christ demands a pollyanna's view of suffering or evil. The cross that mediated the love of God poured forth in our hearts by the Holy Spirit goes to the most tender places of any culture. Nothing in the repertoire of symbols for dealing with pain and failure is more human than the cross, more directly responsive to what people weeping over mangled bodies need to feel. That God could know to the broken bone this human need compounds the mystery of the divine goodness. On the one hand, it leaves unanswered the question of why God should have fashioned creation so that suffering is unavoidable. On the other hand, it stops the whirling mind, the despondent heart, with the solidarity of an embrace, a full fellowship in the painful human condition. What "answer" there is to suffering lies in clouds of unknowing where the cross of Christ becomes acceptable.

Prayer makes the limitations of being human and following a cruciform Lord bearable. When people do manage to end reconciled to their deaths, and their lives, they have surrendered themselves to something of another order, something more significant than humanity. Christians need not blush when explaining their faith, because the One in whom they have placed their trust has done everything one could ask of a savior, and a great deal more.

Summary Reflections II: Relativity, Transcendence, and Action

It remains to ask what the practical effects of meditations such as these on the relativity and transcendence of Christ should be. The first effect that springs to mind is a sense of solidarity with all other people sharing the human condition. For those who penetrate the incarnational center of their Christian faith, what Christians hold in common with other human beings should seem more than enough to overcome fear, alienation, and difference. Each human being is defined by a relation, of dependence and longing, to the sacred mystery Christians call God and others call by other names. Each human being is flesh wanting, needing, to find the spark for its clod, the love that could bring it alive. The love that could bring it alive is an undying love, different from all the perishable loves whose very goodness exacerbates human mortality. The love that could bring our common flesh alive is stronger than evil, as well as death, because when it comes into the human heart it makes enduring evil bearable. Christians are bound to believe that Jesus declares, reveals, exemplifies this love especially acutely, but there is no reason Christians cannot find this love at work all over the globe. Poured forth in the hearts of all who open themselves to it, this love can seem the reason for the Buddha's smile, for Muhammad's great praise of Allah, for the joy of Jewish saints like the Baal Shem Tov.

The actions consequent on appreciating the solidarity of all human beings in the vocation defined by such love can be legion. Most

properly, however, they target the realization, through appropriate economic, legal, political, cultural, religious, and other forms, of structures
that would help human affairs run toward the solidarity implied by the
one human vocation. If all human beings are seeking fulfillment
through the reception of a mysterious love matching the outreach of
their longings and hopes, then all human beings have a basis for mutual
understanding, compassion, and tolerance. Indeed, then it becomes
reasonable to think that all of us human beings are so radically engaged
in a common enterprise that the needs of the many should take priority
over the wants of the few. No one should have the right to luxuries,
superfluities, as long as anyone lacks necessities. Sex, race, age, religion,
occupation, and the other matters that diversify human beings into
potentially antagonistic groups should weigh less than our common
vocation to find and serve the immortalizing divine love.

To be sure, this is more utopian talk, but those who accept the
high christology we have been expounding should not boggle at it. The
politics at which it hints simply extends the Christian view of grace,
which culminates in the notion that the human vocation is to share in
divine life. The Christian warrant for so audacious a notion is the
person and mission of Jesus, perhaps especially his resurrection. No one
knows how to estimate what happened in the resurrection, but every
Christian theologian of sense recognizes that the resurrection launched
the Christian movement. In the risen Christ what had been merely
hopes, hints, wonderful metaphors were swept up into a new symbolism, more objective and of a new order. Some of the contrast appears in
the difference between faith and vision, between grace and glory, between the old eon and the kingdom, the eschaton, the final age. Disciples who were brokenhearted were healed instantaneously. Lives
turned over, careers were abandoned and taken up, the heavens seemed
to have opened and all things to have been made new.

For those able to accept the resurrection of Christ, a politics or
social action predicated on a common human vocation to enter upon
the divine life that is love will not seem outlandish. Rather, it will seem
completely fitting. And despite all the prudence that actual experience
of human nature should inculcate, the person accepting the resurrected Christ has to remain open to the real possibility of human
nature's being transformed. Certainly, the mystery of iniquity continues, as people persist in choosing against the light, against their best
interests, against the only love that might bring them fully alive. Cer-

tainly, the cross of Christ continues to express the pathos of being called to share divine life but so frequently tasting disappointment, pain, abandonment. Yet the cross of Christ cannot be the final word, on Christian grounds. The cross of Christ has to cede to, be fully partnered to, the resurrection of Christ. The good news is that death died, suffering passed over, what had seemed immovable slipped away and heaven replaced the grave.

How should convictions such as these color Christians' interactions with people of other faiths, for instance at occasions of interreligious dialogue? Completely positively. Such other people do not need Christians to convert them to the divine love at work in their hearts. Long before there were Christians the Holy Spirit was working with all people of good will, watering what was arid, washing what was dirtied, taking the smallest openness to the divine mystery as an occasion to instill a desire to abide in the darkness, not flee from the strangeness, let the otherness of God be domesticated, become familiar, at God's own pace. Because early humanity experienced the wonders of nature immediately, early humanity expressed many of its intuitions of the love crucial to its fulfillment in naturalistic terms. The love was like the power of the wind, or the beauty of the jaguar, or the brightening at dawn, or the peace after the storm. Yet even from earliest times some wise people sensed that silence, blankness, solitude, darkness, and other testing areas of human experience and consciousness also were necessary for the intercourse that most set the human heart aflame with holy love. So even from earliest times some brave spirits sought an exodus from the familiar, an alternative to business as usual, a revolt against the giving and taking of pain that could make human life seem a punishment.

Nonetheless, Christ did not simply clarify this universal human condition, though Christians should believe he did that. Christ did not simply enflesh the key struggles for divine love that demarcate the crux of the human vocation. He also set new horizons, most dramatically in loving his enemies, doing good to those who persecuted him, and defeating death by rising to unearthly life. The sense of divinity hinted by the trinitarian symbols that Christ's followers developed was such a fullness of love that he recast the equations in which people had been used to calculating the universal human condition. Christians need not deny that other religious teachers have intuited or even proclaimed similarly new visions. However, they should be forgiven their sense that

Christ accomplished a new creation, because it is at the center of their faith.

What does it mean to act in the grace of Christ's new creation? Only the saints give us a clue. They were sufficiently imbued with the love sought by the human race to illustrate what a transformed humanity, a humanity convinced it was in the midst of a new heaven and a new earth, is like. It is like believing that all creation expresses the divine beauty, is instinct with the divine power. It is like believing that every human being has incalculable worth. It is like grieving at human folly to the point of making one's life a great effort to counteract it. It is like counting earthly goods and accomplishments as straw, compared to the touch of God's love. Each of these "likes" shows the metaphoric character of religious language, rooted in the mysteriousness of religious experience. Each shows the strangeness of acting by virtue of divine love, how the saints skated beyond the boundaries of what the rest of us consider reasonable. For interreligious dialogue, the saints are always daunting. We can be grateful for their flaws, which suggest that peace across religious divisions is more God's doing than something owed to human beings. But we have to be humbled by their ability to live as though the eschaton of God were now, as though the kingdom had come, God's will had been done. Because the Christian saints show what resurrected life can mean, they are a constant reminder that our actions are a function of what we believe God has made possible.

NOTES

1. See 1989 BRITANNICA BOOK OF THE YEAR (Chicago: Encyclopaedia Britannica, 1989), p. 299.

2. Note the Whiteheadean slant toward a pluralist ontology in John B. Cobb, Jr.'s otherwise admirably confessional study, "Toward a Christocentric Catholic Theology," in TOWARD A UNIVERSAL THEOLOGY OF RELIGION, ed. Leonard Swidler (Maryknoll, N.Y.: Orbis, 1987), pp. 86–100.

3. There is an interesting tension between the views of Leonard Swidler ("Interreligious and Interideological Dialogue: The Matrix for All Systematic Reflection Today") and Raimundo Panikkar ("The Invisible Harmony: A Universal Theory of Religion or a Cosmic Confidence in Reality?"). See ibid., pp. 5–50 and 118–153. Note also the attempt of Thomas Dean ("Universal Theology and Dialogical Dialogue") to reconcile the two (ibid., pp. 162–174).

4. William Thompson's side of a debate with Swidler and John Hick sug-

gests the differences that a formal commitment to orthodox Christology can create. See William M. Thompson, Leonard Swidler, and John Hick, "Editorial Symposium," HORIZONS, 16/1 (Spring, 1989), 101–130.

5. See Rosemary Radford Ruether, "Feminism and Jewish-Christian Dialogue," and Marjorie Hewitt Suchocki, "In Search of Justice," in John Hick and Paul F. Knitter, eds., THE MYTH OF CHRISTIAN UNIQUENESS (Maryknoll, N.Y.: Orbis, 1987), pp. 137–148 and 149–161. See also Elsa Tamez, ed., THROUGH HER EYES: WOMEN'S THEOLOGY FROM LATIN AMERICA (Maryknoll, N.Y.: Orbis, 1989).

6. Tom F. Driver, "The Case for Pluralism," in THE MYTH OF CHRISTIAN UNIQUENESS, pp. 203–218.

7. Our view opposes that of Hans Küng in his otherwise admirable essay, "Christianity and World Religions: Dialogue with Islam," in TOWARD A UNIVERSAL THEOLOGY OF RELIGION, pp. 192–209. One of the best Catholic theological studies of the world religions is Küng's CHRISTIANITY AND THE WORLD RELIGIONS (Garden City, N.Y.: Doubleday, 1986).

Chapter 4

How Christ Is Unique

Religious Unity

We have considered some of the arguments against the uniqueness of Christ, often finding them stimuli to reassert Christian convictions that Jesus had words of eternal life not available elsewhere. Accepting the premise that the religious life of humankind shows considerable diversity, we reflected on why this fact should cause Christians to trim their claims for Jesus—and why it need not. In the present chapter we consider arguments for the uniqueness of Christ, many of them related to the similarities running through the world religions. Here the basic intuition will be that what Christ experienced and taught has a universal quality, making him an archetype or everyman. Perhaps paradoxically, much of his uniqueness shines forth in the degree to which he recapitulates the sufferings and hopes of human beings the world over. No one ever spoke as he had, Christians have long believed, because he was speaking God's privileged words of salvation—words applicable to Gentiles as well as Jews, to Asians as well as Europeans.

From the perspective of Christian faith, humankind displays a notable religious unity because everywhere people are involved in the same basic situation. Everywhere, divinity only appears mysteriously. Everywhere, human beings reach out for a fulfillment that space and time do not allow. So, all human beings depend on the grace of their creator. For people to find meaning, maintain hope, end their days with the conviction that they have experienced more good than bad, the mysteriousness of their situation has to have made itself congenial. What parents have found in the tough hours of early morning, tending a sick child, has to have become privileged: trust is possible, there is no real alternative to going on. Similarly, what lovers have found in their

82

conjugal embrace, artists have found in creative work, scientists have found pursuing understanding has to have become privileged: the world is an amazing place, much better than we have any right to expect.

Human beings share all the crucial experiences. All are born small, defenseless, needy, and ignorant. All have to learn how to make their way in the world. All have to negotiate some separation from the family life, or the lack of family life, that shaped their first years. Through the adult years, all have to lick the wounds caused by physical pain, injustice, worry about the morrow. Equally, all have to cherish the good times, the beautiful hours, and think about what they mean. Finally, all have to die, taking their leave of the only existence they knew and making their peace with the grave. All have to wonder whether anything lies after death—what they should believe. So one can sketch the same basic trajectory for all human beings, and the common denominator all the way through is not knowing. None of us knows the beginning, or the foundation, or the beyond of our existence, our selves. Commonly, as a fate that could make us compassionate as well as wise, we have to act without knowing, to love without seeing, to live by faith. The just person lives by faith. The person who gives bedrock reality its due embraces life's mysteriousness.

Does this mean that it makes no difference whether one is a man or a woman, an Asian or an African, a child or an adult, a beggar or a prince? Not at all. Sex, race, age, and economic station all color the mysteriousness of the human condition, varying it the way a kaleidoscope varies certain basic patterns. If mystery is the light common to all human lives, sex, race, age, and economic station are prisms, angling that light now this way and now that. So we are back to the ancient perception of the one and the many. We are even back to the perennial perception that people are alike in being unique, united in being varied. For many of the most significant religious judgments, however, the unity of human beings in face of divine mystery ought to weigh heavier than the variety of human beings in face of diverse cultural situations.

Only a very few religious geniuses have fashioned truly universal ways of dealing with divine mystery, as the consensus of humanity about the axial figures of world history suggests. Only a handful of names draw two percent or more (100 million) of the world's population to inscribe themselves as believers. Jesus, Muhammad, Krishna, the Buddha, Confucius, Lao Tzu, and perhaps Karl Marx are the obvious figures with whom one has to reckon, if the question is how today's billions cope with divine mystery. Certainly, historical considerations suggest the significance of Moses and Paul, Socrates and Darwin, Einstein and Freud. But even with the addition of such other figures the list of truly crucial figures remains small. The main characteristic of the great religious figures on this list is that they articulated a comprehensive view of reality. The mysterious ultimate they reverenced brought order to nature, society, and individual alike. By reaching attunement with the Tao, or Allah, or the functional equivalent in other systems, one could gain basic human health.

The struggle for basic human health seems to be another universal. The world over, human beings are alike in wanting their bodies, minds, spirits, groups, and habitats to flourish. Conversely, they are alike in fighting sickness in any of these areas. So they have bent might and main to ward off disease, dispel ignorance, defeat malice, overthrow injustice, and restore or flee damaged ecospheres. The common human struggling with mystery has included a tiring fight against many things that people knew in their bones ought not to have been. Disease ought not to have been, because health seemed normal, to be taken for granted, while sickness seemed puzzling, extraordinary. Malice ought not to have been, because it threw all human relations out of joint, setting brother against brother and friend against friend. And so with the other great burdens: stupidity, natural disaster, death. The experience of any of these realities carried with it a shaking of the head, a revolt of the will, a soul-deep resentment. Certainly, wisdom entailed some reconciliation to the inevitability of stupidity, malice, and above all death. Certainly, there were naive and sophisticated forms of resentment. But resentment there was, and the most influential religious seers turned this resentment into an intuition of transcendence. The key thing about the human person was his or her potential to escape what ought not to be.

Christ, our main focus in this study, made conversion to the good news of the Father's kingdom the gateway to escaping what ought not to be. If people would turn around, have a change of heart, they could get the better of sickness, ignorance, malice, social disorder, and even natural disaster. Their turning around, going in a different direction, could connect them with a power, a love, more basic, more real, than any of the disorders, the should-not-be's, afflicting them. Living by faith in God, rather than by the opinions of their group or self-reliance, they could escape the prison of this-worldly, historical expectations and possibilities.

Buddhism has penetrated the west slightly in recent generations. Christianity has penetrated all but the Asian cultures significantly in recent centuries. Islam is on the move, widening its influence. Each of these huge religious complexes has a persuasive view of the unity of humankind. Each thinks that all human beings, regardless of sex, race, age, or locale, fit its prescription for curing sickness and creating health. So leading representatives of the diverse religious traditions themselves agree about the profound likeness of human beings. When it comes to assessing the basic situation in which members of our species exist, Buddhist detachment, Muslim submission, and Christian love all claim to be medicinal or saving. Clearly, therefore, pluralism about humanity's views of salvation is not the only word. Clearly, much unity is also at work, suggesting that at the bedrock of the religious experience human beings are unified by the objective priority of sacred mystery.

The Infinity of Christianity

Because Christianity is an affair of human beings and history, it is limited in its ability to express the divinity working for all people's salvation. Because Christianity is an affair of Father, Son, and Spirit, it stands outside of history, escaping the historicist's dogmas about limitation. Christian theologians are right to stress the historical specificity of Jesus. From earliest times, Christians had to fight the tendency to make Jesus a mythic figure—one who did not really suffer and die, one whose every action was controlled by God like a puppet. In saying that Jesus was fully human, Christian faith rejected this mythologizing and kept its feet squarely on historical ground. On the other hand, from equally early times Christian theologians were convinced that the actions of Christ that accomplished salvation were the effects of the divine Logos and extended to all people. Christ died once and for all. People who never heard of Christ, or had not yet been born, or had died long before him all benefited from his actions, because they all belonged to the one human race and he was its head, its new Adam.

When we reflect on the infinity of Christianity, so as to force historicists to qualify their delimitations of what Christ can be, we depend on the divinity of Jesus. If there were no divine Word in his depths, Jesus Christ would not be uniquely universal. However much we say that this Word gave the act of existence to a full human being, we are still going to encounter skepticism. "It isn't possible to affirm the Logos in Christ without forfeiting his humanity," many are going to say. "He can't really be like us if he was the Son of God." But traditional Christian faith, interpreting the New Testament, the earliest liturgical usages, and the conciliar and patristic teachings, denies this reasoning. Inseparable from traditional Christian faith is the scandal we have mentioned: the twofold assertion that Christ is both fully human and fully divine.

Claims that Christianity is infinite are tarred with this scandal. To say that what Christians celebrate as good news applies to all people can offend non-Christians, because it can seem to be telling non-Christians that Christians know better than they what their condition actually is. (We can bracket the issue of putative Christians themselves being scandalized by the claim that the good news applies to all people, regardless of whether they have formally accepted Christ or not. That is largely, though not entirely, a defect of fundamentalism.) And even when it is admitted that Buddhists or Hindus or Muslims have their own versions of such universal claims, now more and now less genteel than the Christian claims, the Christian notion of universal grace can still rankle. Ultimately, Christians can only try to explain their views and let the chips fall where they may.

Late in his ecumenical career, after his notion of anonymous Christians was well known, the great Catholic theologian Karl Rahner met a prominent Buddhist. The Buddhist allowed that Rahner's idea made considerable sense: from a Christian's standpoint, the holiness manifest in the life of an exemplary Buddhist would have to be due to Christ, and so it would be fitting to call such a Buddhist an anonymous Christian. However, what would Rahner make of a Buddhist asserting a complementary claim? How would he receive the notion that, from a Buddhist standpoint, the good Christian is an anonymous Buddhist? Rahner answered that he completely accepted the proposition. Granted the differences in the two frames of reference, each had the right to interpret all relevant data according to its own criteria and name them as it found best.[1]

Rahner left for another day the question of whether both frames of reference can be legitimate. He did not enter into the hard work of trying to determine where the two systems do and do not agree in their interpretations of human experience, and so he left hanging what mutuality the two different interpretations might enjoy. Today those discussing religion across the world's great traditions are drawing closer to such mutuality, though they are far from having fashioned the tools the full task will require. For our purposes, however, the legitimacy that Rahner and his Buddhist counterpart accorded one another's efforts to understand all people's experiences according to their own categories is instructive. That is all we are attempting right now: to make sense in Christian terms of the grace apparent in the lives of non-Christians. The corollary is a willingness to let others make sense of our experience in their Buddhist, Muslim, or other non-Christian categories.

Two points remain. The first is to advance the idea, latent in the mention of mutuality, that it is not enough to explain people only in one's own categories. One must also let people explain themselves as they see fit and allow their self-explanations to impinge on one's own categories. The second point is that some aspects of one's categories cannot be changed, as long as one maintains orthodox christology. Christ is always going to be the savior of all humankind, unless one breaks with the faith long handed down and adulterates the key Christian concepts.

Granted this, what does it mean for Christ to be the savior of all humankind, the central channel of the grace that divinizes any person saying a radical yes to the divine mystery? (Human gropings naturally stumble, but let us think hard about this question.) It means that Jesus Christ somehow possessed or gathered into himself the core of being human. When he opened this core to divinity, in the uniquely intimate way consequent on the hypostatic union (the incarnation of the Logos), humanity itself was changed. This change did not take away the freedom of individual men and women. They retained the power to accept or reject the divine offer of divinizing love. But in and through Jesus God put into human affairs the power to escape from all the dysfunctions that had mottled the human condition. In the love that Jesus incarnated, expressed, and made a factor in all of human history, God redid the human situation. The human situation was now radically a success rather than radically a failure, because now it had achieved the one thing for which it had been made: union with the Infinite in love.

Because of the solidarity among all human beings, their sharing the same condition and being connected to one another by lines of genetic and historical influence, the achievement in Jesus of the one thing for which human nature had been made was an achievement in principle for all. For the mind and plan and love of God, which exist apart from time and contemplate creation as a whole, Jesus appears as the nodal point, the hub, of the concert of actions by which God has chosen to make and guide a world. This is the intuition we find in the prologue of John's gospel, where the Word that became flesh in Christ was that in whom all things were made. This is the intuition of Colossians 1:17: "He is before all things, and in him all things hold together." The actions in time of this extra-temporal source of the world's unity acquire a formative quality. It is they that give time, history, its basic structure, when one approaches history from the horizon of Christian faith. The actions of Christ expressed and shared the love that united humanity to divinity definitively and so secured the human venture in success. "Salvation" considered negatively is the removal of what impedes human health. Considered positively it is the securing of the human venture in success, the divinization of human beings in love. Because of Christians' faith that Jesus was the personal place where humanity came to know its vocation to divinization, Christians are bound to consider Jesus the universal savior. The love that the Father, Son, and Spirit offer those who abide in Christ has parallels in Hinduism and Islam, perhaps also in Buddhism, but its Christian overtones remain distinct: more intimate and incarnational. Judaism may well speak of virtually the same divine offer, and the same loving substance, but Judaism has shied away from claiming "divinization," as well as from the trinitarian structure of people's abiding in grace and the centering of this whole soteriological complex in Jesus Christ. Thus the Christian sense of the infinity of Christ's work and movement is unique.

Death as a Common Pressure

The greatest pressure to think about salvation in these universal terms is death, our common human fate. Christianity claims that Christ conquered death. Using the two dominant symbols from its original cultural milieu, resurrection of the body and immortality of the soul, Christianity made clear from earliest times that the victory it attributed to Jesus went to the taproots of the human condition and tore out the oldest enemy. In what sense did Christ save humanity from death? In the sense that his resurrection became more basic and central. Although human beings would continue to die, death would not have the final say in their significance. Jesus had died, most horribly, but in raising Jesus the Father had shown that the love on which Jesus had gambled was stronger than death. The resurrection was both the Father's definitive ratification of Jesus' message and person and the inauguration of a new state of affairs. Call that new state of affairs the kingdom, or the new creation, or the eschatological era, its basic import remained the same. The door that death previously had slammed shut against human significance now was cast open. The futility that had haunted human existence now was swept aside. In their experience of the risen Lord, the early Christians learned immediately, with no need for argument, that their lives were surpassingly significant. As a consummate act of mercy, God had made the cruelest portion of the human condition a conduit to complete fulfillment.

Indeed, the more that the earliest Christians contemplated the significance of the resurrection of Christ and the sending of the Spirit symbolized at Pentecost, the more they saw that death had been made penultimate and instrumental, because the very life of God had replaced death as humanity's first principle. Jesus had been resurrected because his union with the Father was so intimate that the deathlessness of the Father had become his own. For Greek thought, the difference between divinity and humanity was precisely the deathlessness of the divine and the mortality of the human. Jesus had bridged this gap, canceled out this difference. By taking humanity into divinity, God had made human beings partakers of the divine deathlessness, the divine eternity.

Now, other religious traditions have spoken of immortality and resurrection. Eastern traditions have spoken of divinization, usually in the sense of dissolving at death and becoming part of the eternal cosmos (the best symbol of divinity). But the resurrection of Christ was something new and unique. Here was the "return," for a brief while, of a fully historical human being, transformed by his entrance into the divine state but still recognizable. Here was a symbolism, rooted in the actual experiences of such prominent early Christians as Magdalene, Peter, John, the other apostles, Paul, and many others, proclaiming the radical transformation of the historical, bodily, recognizably here-and-now human condition. Just as the incarnation put into ordinary human affairs divinity-enfleshed, so the resurrection put into the space-time experience of representative human beings a foretaste of a new human destiny.

It doesn't matter that no one, including the New Testament authors, has been able to understand the resurrection of Christ. It doesn't matter that almost by definition the resurrection of Christ eludes the parameters we customarily use to describe historical events: "real" in contrast to "mythic" or "imaginary" happenings. Even when one has shown that the contrasts among such entities as "history," "reality," "myth," and "imagination" are slippery, something scandalous remains. By now we should be familiar with such scandal. It attaches to every crucial Christian claim, because every crucial Christian claim is a window onto the divine mystery that Jesus incarnated. But one can no more eviscerate Christian faith of the resurrection than one can eviscerate it of the divinity of Christ. Take away the resurrection and Christians are of all people the most to be pitied. Paul thought this, because Paul wanted his converts to sacrifice this-worldly pleasures and live as though heaven (a resurrected existence) were their true home. It is hard to present oneself as a faithful Christian and disagree with Paul on this point.

Which again brings us back to the question of the authorities among which one must choose. Why should Paul, or other New Testament sources, or long-standing Christian liturgical practice rank higher than present-day critics who cannot accept the resurrection, or the incarnation that a high christology affirms, or divinization, or the Trinity, or any of the other cardinal Christian mysteries (including the mystery that God should have given salvation the structure that biblical faith claims God did)? This is the question constantly put to those in the middle of debates such as the one we have entered, and we continue to underscore the existential cut of it. What finally is at stake is the way to live, the personal option, the inalienable stance one takes in view of death, evil, potential meaninglessness, and all their positive countervalents. What is the experiential basis, the beauty, the coherence, the viability, of the alternatives one is being offered? On the one hand, there is the Christian vision, rooted in long-standing memories of Jesus Christ, claimed to be validated by saints and mystics galore, elaborated by formidable thinkers into a comprehensive statement about how to cure humanity's ills and assure humanity's dazzling success. On the other hand (if one is fortunate enough to get from the critic a positive alternative thorough enough to be called a worldview), there is something different, which usually makes lesser claims and holds out dimmer prospects. We find no parity between the authority implied (only occasionally put forth) by those who would restrict the significance of Christ and those myriad exemplary Christians who have been willing to die for their conviction that Christ alone had done the one thing necessary: given humanity its definitive victory and success. For us the two visions are almost laughably incomparable.

This does not mean critics have nothing to say, past formulations of Christian convictions are completely adequate, popular Christian faith hasn't abused orthodox views of the incarnation, Christians haven't failed regularly to be the good exemplars and neighbors their faith demanded of them. It does not mean that today's awareness of the depth and beauty of several, perhaps many, other worldviews shouldn't be taken into account. It simply means that the bottom line continues to be the need of limited human beings (none of whom has ever seen God, all of whose lives are short) to make sense, here and now, of a world always mysterious and often threatening to crush them. One doesn't give up a vision, a faith, precious because of its apparent truth and its obvious power to carry people through life's greatest challenges, simply because a new historical situation poses some new questions. All the more so is this the case when it remains to be proved that any of these new questions impugns the core of such a vision.

Let us take the common pressure of death as a grace, a much needed reminder to be fully serious (though never grim) when we do theology. Let us take the controversies about the significance of Christ, like the controversies about proper memorials at places like Auschwitz, to renew our appreciation of how precious the traditions and symbols by which different peoples have kept faith with the divine mystery always should seem. Arguably, there is no set of symbols that has done more to help human beings find their lives bearable, even joyous, than the symbols generated by Jesus Christ. Even when one accepts the dolorous counter-suggestion, that there is no set of symbols that has been more viciously abused, to humanity's great hurt, the seriousness of tampering with the key Christian convictions remains. Of course, we have to "tamper" with what we have been taught about Christ, about salvation, about grace, if we are to appropriate our tradition and bring it to bear on present problems. But we should always do this with great reverence, begging God's help to walk the fine line between a paralyzing fear of making mistakes and a precipitous jettisoning of treasures we had too little appreciated. Otherwise, we may cede to some amorphous "universal theology" the vision that our predecessors in the passionate love of Jesus deemed unsurpassable.

Christ as Icon

Taking up the question of the unsurpassability of Christ, Paul Knitter has described letting go of special claims for Jesus (so that Jesus and Muhammad or Jesus and the Buddha might stand on the same level) as a "Rubicon" standing before those serious about interreligious dialogue. Specifically, he has urged Hans Küng, whom he has found bold in urging Christians to grant Muhammad the status of a great prophet, to cross this Rubicon and give up the language about the definitive, unsurpassable character of God's revelation in Christ that Küng has regularly employed. For his part, Küng seems reluctant to take such a step, apparently identifying the commitment that makes him a Christian with some such belief that Jesus is unique.[2]

In our view, Küng is quite correct, though he has not grounded his position as solidly as he could and should have. For Küng regularly elaborates a christology that stresses God's instrumental use of the humanity of Jesus, without adding the balancing statements about the divinity of Christ that the full tradition has employed. In a word, Küng's christology is usually "low," not in the sense that he specifically denies the divinity of Christ, but in the sense that he concentrates upon the humanity. Relatedly, he displays an aversion for "Greek" views of Jesus and prefers "Jewish" views. This allows him to establish common cause with Jews and Muslims on many points, but it provides critics such as Knitter valid grounds for asking why he does not see or follow through upon the apparent logic of his own position. Either he should deny the high christology associated with the "Greek" component of the New Testament and early Christian patrimony, or he should shore up his statements about the unsurpassable, definitive character of what God did in Christ by grounding them in the strict divinity of the Word that took flesh in Christ, the ontological person that Jesus Christ was.

Küng is more than capable of explaining his own christology, however, so it is more fitting for us to meditate passingly about this "Greek" component of Christian tradition that so regularly is disparaged. Indeed, although Eastern Orthodox Christians have an admirable record in Christian ecumenism, having long been members of the World Council of Churches, their relative absence from interreligious dialogue has been an impoverishment. When Orthodox Christians are present, the sacramentality of the traditional christology shines with greater luster. As a result, the passionate love of Christ that we placed at the foundations of Catholic Christian spirituality comes into view, making Christian reservations about a universal theology (one that would place all religious traditions on an equal footing) seem healthy rather than hidebound.[3]

There are ways in which all religious traditions should be placed on an equal footing. The primary such way is to take what human beings actually experience and accomplish as data for God's widespread work in the world, and to give no religious group privileged status as morally superior. No individuals are necessarily closer to God or human perfection than any other individuals, simply because their group feels "chosen" or graced. Christians are as admirable in their humanity as what Christians do. The same for Buddhists, Jews, Muslims, Hindus, and any other groups. There are Christian saints and Christian sinners. The same with all other groups. Morally, the proof of the pudding is in the eating, and so focusing on such moral matters as the deeds of holiness, the political ways and means of liberation, and the present imperatives of justice is the safest, most useful angle that interreligious discussions can take (for the foreseeable future).

However, when one comes to existential theology—one's passionate faith seeking understanding—the angle that one must take in interpreting the full range of data provided by humanity's historical experience (which includes religion, along with all the other vehicles of searching and self-expression) is confessional. It is where one has placed one's life's meaning that should determine one's horizon. Otherwise, one is schizophrenic and violates the key existential precept that purity of heart is to will one thing.

The Christ seizing the heart of Catholic spirituality, east and west, is the icon of God. Roman Catholics have made this clear in their sacramentality, but eastern Christians have made it even clearer in their worship, theology, and spirituality. And what does it mean for Christ to be the icon of God? It means that the same humanity of Jesus that Jewish Christian theology stressed so validly is transparent for divinity. It means that Christ, without ceasing to be the particular man Jesus of Nazareth, is the great metaphor of God. As patristic theology put it, Christ is the image of the image. If the Logos is the image of God, then Jesus Christ, the Logos enfleshed, is what the Logos can be in human terms. We alluded to some of the richness of this iconic, sacramental, metaphorical dimension of Christ when dealing with spiritual absorption with the biblical scenes as fathomless mysteries. Christ on the cross, Jesus turning the water into wine, Jesus multiplying the loaves and fishes, Jesus forgiving the woman taken in adultery—for faith all of these scenes have a depth and resonance that is inexhaustible. Each of them reflects the consummate mystery that in space and time the eternal self-expression of the Father drew away what it could of the veil (the darkness) intrinsic to divinity and pitched its tent in our human midst. One might call this the divine poetry, or the divine iconography, or the divine dramaturgy—any of the terms suggesting a work of art applies, and none captures the whole. The whole is more original. It is from the enfleshment of the Logos that western culture (world culture?) gets its best tutoring in the potential of humanity to mediate divinity, just as it is from the enfleshment of the Logos that western culture (world culture?) gets its most profound understanding of comedy and knows why the human venture is not a tragedy.

The iconic appreciation of Jesus Christ is not prominent in the presentations of the majority of Christian theologians active in interreligious dialogue. Whether by temperament or from doctrinal conviction, most of those sympathetic to non-Christian religions and wanting to establish common ground with them are not proponents of a high christology. In the terms used earlier, they are "Jewish" rather than "Greek." This is a pity, not because the "Jewish" stress on the humanity of Christ is invalid, but because the "Greek" stress offers equally rich grounds for appreciating non-Christian religious achievements.

One can argue, perhaps tendentiously, that the iconic view of Christ so marries the best of the low and high christologies (rivets so exactly at the center of the incarnational mystery) that it gives non-Christian partners to interreligious dialogue the best possible value.

That is to say, one can argue that the iconic christology is more faithful to the full, Catholic tradition than the alternatives and so is a better representative of Christian faith than the alternatives. This is an argument to be joined by Christians themselves—a dispute to be settled from inside the Christian camp.

One can also argue, however, that the infinity of the Logos, its correlation with wisdom wherever found, places adherents of an iconic christology in a better position to appreciate the splendor of the Buddha, of Muhammad, of Lao Tzu than where adherents of a low christology are placed. We shall develop this thesis in the next section. Here it is enough to point out that the "Greek" understanding of Jesus Christ has always made him the Pantokrator, the Ruler of All. If one can strip this term of its pejoratively imperial overtones (and we shall argue that one can), it implies that the Logos Christians worship (as both uncreated and enfleshed) has been present wherever human beings have developed a profound humanity: great wisdom and love, great creativity and endurance of suffering.

What the Buddha and Muhammad Did Not Claim

The doctrine of the Pantokrator stresses the universal presence and rule of the Logos. Whether one speaks of physical nature or human nature, the expression of the Father is the pattern, the matrix, within which intelligibility occurs. As long as one accepts the Catholic Christian position that God is light in whom there is no darkness at all (a position that some eastern philosophies may oppose), for something to exist is for that something to be intelligible by virtue of the Logos.

The unique feature of this Christian view of the foundations of reality is that it makes human flesh the prime metaphor of universal intelligibility. If Jesus is the icon of the Logos, then what was revealed in and through Jesus has pride of place. This does not mean that natural revelation—what the physical universe suggests—has no value. Because Jesus was truly human, he was limited, and so what he could reveal of the Logos, of God, was limited. But it does mean that revelation has a certain irremovable anthropocentrism. If one confesses the incarnation, one's world pivots on what was revealed through the human flesh of Christ. This confession should be chastened by what the physical sciences tell us about the natural world. It offers no justification for raping nature. And it has to be correlated with the several ways in which the Christian view of reality also makes it theocentric—the several ways in which the infinity of God, spilling over even its iconic vessel, retains a priority. (There is the problem of how to speak about this infinite, "excessive" reality making the universe theocentric, but that need not detain us here.) Nonetheless, the Christian claim and gamble is that the love revealed in Christ is the best analogy for the divine nature. God is love (*agape*), and Christ gives Christians their best understanding of love. The love of Christ best shows "what" God is, how God thinks, what God is doing in the world.

This said, what are the implications for Christians' views of other great religious figures, such as the Buddha and Muhammad? No doubt the implications are several, but the following most lure us into reflection. First, the wisdom of the Buddha, which focused on removing desire and egocentricity, seems a luminous expression of the truth that Christians attribute to the Logos. In teaching people to stop craving worldly goods, to stop clinging even to their sense of personal identity, the Buddha clarified the priority of a reality transcending the world and the human self. How one should understand such "transcendence" is a challenging question. Much in Buddhism insists that there is no ultimate reality standing apart from what human beings know as the world, no independent being on the order of the Hindu Brahman undergirding what one might call the phenomenal realm. The point of stopping desire is to see the interconnected, concatenated nature of reality. The individual items (*dharmas*) constituting reality form a stream, a flux, something to which the wise cannot cling. The nirvana that brings one release from the imprisoning character of the dharmas does not stand apart from them as a solid Other. Rather, it is their reality perceived without clinging—the dark light that shines when the flame of desire has been snuffed out.

One may consider this so much esoteric poetry, but only at the price of failing to appreciate the depths to which the human mind must go when it wants to grapple with the question of how the world is founded, how God and the world relate. For Christians, the Father is divinity beyond which one cannot go, divinity as unoriginated or self-causing. The Logos is the expression of the Father. Within the godhead, the Logos is the only begotten of the Father, the "Word" that comes forth when the Father "speaks" (thinks, communicates). The Spirit is their love, "rounding out" their perfect mutuality. Outside of the godhead, in creation, the Logos is credited with the intelligibility that grounds whatever exists. Christian theology is bound to think of the universe as finite. Otherwise, Christian theology would have to consider the universe as strictly divine. The universe therefore is only a partial reflection of or participation in the being whose intelligibility Christian faith associates with the Logos. At the point where existence and intelligibility coincide, the Logos is the "reason" for the world. To human beings this point may seem an asymtote—a far point of convergence never actually seen. When one tries to strip away the effects of human limitation, however, it becomes likely that, for God, to be and to be intelligible, to be "mental" light, are one and the same. The Buddha sensed this. Even more, he sensed the moral conditions necessary for appreciating so foundational a truth and receiving the freedom it offers. So the Buddha bears a likeness to Christ in having been a vehicle of profound revelation. It makes sense, then, to credit the Buddha, his teaching, and the achievements of his followers to the Logos, the Pantokrator ruling over the ultimate arrangements of creation, the ultimate coincidence of being and light.

The Buddha did not claim that love is the best index of the divine nature. He did not make human flesh the signal metaphor of ultimate reality. His wisdom was healing, saving, but not in the agonized mode of Christ's cross. There was no resurrection tying his way inextricably to human flesh. His way was not radically incarnational (though it was beautifully humanistic and his followers have often been wonderful iconographers). So his expression of the Logos differed from that of Christ, and his followers by and large did not claim for him the sort of union between flesh and Logos that the followers of Christ claimed for their Lord.

Neither Muhammad nor his followers claimed that human flesh is the privileged metaphor of divinity. Indeed, they denied that God has a Son, any sort of sharer of divinity. The Word of God, addressed to human beings and (for many Muslims) existing with Allah eternally, is the Qur'an. The Qur'an is what happened when Allah spoke definitively to human beings. Thus, the Qur'an holds the place in Islam that Jesus Christ, the Logos enfleshed, holds in Christianity. Much as Islam abhors representations of God, thinking them idolatrous, it reveres the Qur'an as the privileged place where divinity becomes "available." Relatedly, it reveres Muhammad as the exemplary respondent to God, the complete Muslim. The Qur'an and Muhammad therefore both carry metaphoric valence. Both point beyond themselves and "incarnate" divinity (in an accommodated sense).

For Christians, Muhammad seems like a great prophet, announcing such crucial truths as the oneness of God, the imminence of divine judgment, the propensity of human beings to forget their Lord and so become unrealistic. In the prophecy of Muhammad sympathetic Christians are bound to find the work of the Logos, articulating the basic structures of the human condition, and the work of the Spirit, moving human beings to accept God. The holiness of numerous Muslim saints only compounds this impression. For those with eyes of faith, it is obvious that grace has abounded in Sufi brotherhoods, numerous mosques, and many ordinary Muslim families. Whatever quarrels Christians may have with Muslim notions of law (*shariah*), politics, warfare, and the like, Christians should confess their admiration of Islam's great cultural (spiritual) achievements before entering into criticism.

How significant is it that Muhammad did not stress love, or mount a cross, or forgive sins, or speak to God like a child to its parent, the way that Jesus did? For Christians, very significant. Inasmuch as Christians account such things important parts of the revelation and incarnation of God they believe paradigmatic and definitive, Muhammad's missing such traits qualifies his prophecy considerably.

Lastly, what should we say to those who complain that we have misrepresented the Buddha or Muhammad, and that our approach to them has been twisted by our Christian commitments? We should say that we will gladly be corrected, when we offer descriptions of non-Christian traditions that adherents of those traditions consider inaccurate or distorting. We should also say that we cannot rid ourselves of our Christian commitments when we try to estimate the ultimate significance of non-Christian religious phenomena, and that we cannot cede to outsiders the judgments about such ultimate significance that Christian faith requires of us. If we say that Buddhists believe such and such, and Buddhists tell us that they do not, we should withdraw our statement. If we say that for Christian faith, as we hold it, the Buddha reflects the Logos best revealed in Jesus Christ, Buddhists do not have the authority to gainsay us. They may say they do not understand us, or that our categories do not fit how they have understood their experience, and we should rethink our interpretations in light of their responses. But we finally have to make sense of the Buddha or Muhammad on our own grounds, as functions of the Christ who is our alpha and omega. Otherwise, we are not making our determinations of ultimate reality from our Christian faith.

Christ in Western History

To the mind of the Christian theologian, Christ has given western history its deepest humanism. The portrait of Jesus developed in the gospels has provided the most influential model of what it means to be a human being. Recently Aloysius Pieris has challenged the usual acceptance of the terms "western" and "eastern," pointing out that Indian thought is closer to Greek thought than is Semitic thought. Pieris therefore proposes taking "eastern" to mean "oriented to wisdom" and "western" to mean "oriented to love."[4] This is a proposal with considerable merit, but it does not negate the fact that Christian humanism most fully took hold in the European cultures, and that for them Christ was the embodiment of both wisdom and love. Indeed, Christ was the embodiment of the divine gamble that supreme wisdom is so loving toward the world as to give the only begotten Son for its salvation.

It is a nice question whether the religious traditions customarily considered eastern (Hinduism, Buddhism, Confucianism, Taoism) understand this divine gamble. They can answer for themselves, all the more so since it is questionable that many Europeans or Americans have understood it. What does it mean to say that Christ represents the divine love poured out for the salvation of human beings? What ought one to hear when the gospel stories, the crucifixion of Christ, and Christ's resurrection are read as variations on that theme?

First, one ought to hear news so good as to be hard to accredit. As many have noted, the problem with the gospel is that we human beings find it difficult to believe that God could be as good as the Father of Jesus is portrayed. Certainly, we understand the logic of *a fortiori* playing in such statements of Jesus as, "What father among you, if his son asks for a fish, will instead of a fish give him a serpent; or if he asks for an egg, will give him a scorpion? If you then, who are evil, know how to give good gifts to your children, how much more will the heavenly Father give the Holy Spirit to those who ask him?" (Lk 11:11–13). But we hesitate to apply the entire soteriological work of Jesus to ourselves. Could it in fact be that God so loved *us* that Jesus did what he did, suffered what he suffered, for us and our salvation?

This loving intention of the Father motivating all the words, deeds, sufferings, and triumphs of Jesus does not make the life of Jesus less human than it would have been without the Father's will. It makes the life of Jesus more human. That is the point to observations such as Karl Rahner's that closeness to God increases the individuality of the creature. That is the lesson one finds in the lives of the saints, whose prayer and loving service of their fellow human beings sculpt them to great originality. So the obedience that Jesus showed was a path to consummate originality and achievement. The love on which God gambled was the source of the most inspiring figure the west has ever celebrated.

Still, more remains to be asked. How did this love accomplish salvation? What do we believe about God, by virtue of Jesus' dying and rising for humanity's sake? This love accomplished salvation by making divinity a partaker of human travail. It overcame the deepest alienations of humanity by mediating God's rapture of humanity into the divine embrace. When God replaced human mortality with the divine deathlessness, humanity entered into a heritage it hadn't known was possible. The divine love that Jesus expressed and made the most potent energy in creation (as the resurrection testified) healed humanity by uniting it with unfailing health: divinity itself.

In the humanism of the west shaped by Christian faith, the summit of the achievement to which men and women could aspire was to become useful servants of God's saving love. Human perfection was a function of creative, selfless love. The more that people caused life, joy, peace, and goodness to flourish, the more they imitated their divine source, followed Jesus their Lord, and fulfilled the potential God had breathed into their souls. Adherents of the Asian religions can speak about the parallels they find in the vow of the bodhisattva to labor for the salvation of all living things, or in the premier Confucian virtue of *jen* (love, fellow-feeling). To an outsider, however, it seems that a different dynamic is at work. In Asia, love on the sacrificial model of Jesus has not been the prime analogue of divinity. Flesh torn for the sake of fellow human beings has not hung over the altar, telling all worshipers that the path by which divinity chose to save human beings was cruciform.

The instinct to impose the law of the cross as the basic law of redemption, east and west, runs into the complexity that we noted above. One can only make the law of the cross statutory for non-Christians by arguing on specifically Christian grounds, in an effort to make sense of all human experience in Christian terms. The result should be a keen sense of the humility with which Christian interpretations of such phenomena as caste, racism, sexism, and other prominent features of non-Christian cultures should be tendered. It is not enough to say from the beginning that the western cultures shaped by Christianity have their own obvious failings, many perhaps greater than the failings of the east. One must also say that one's interpretational stance depends upon the iconic Christ—in this case the Christ whose hanging from the cross represents a great victory.

It would improve most interreligious dialogues if the participants paid more attention to the crucified Christ and sought his equivalents in the other traditions than they do customarily. It would profit ordinary believers more if the basic statuary of the different traditions were juxtaposed, in an effort to suggest what in fact has been the great beauty, the primal allure, that has drawn the mainstream of believers to the savior in question. There is an acuteness to the crucified Christ that cuts through most academic verbiage. There is, or should be, an existential urgency that forces people to say what in fact they hold most dear, what they just might be willing to die for. No doubt the western cultures have produced myriad heroes and models, but it is not hard to argue that Jesus Christ puts all the rest in the shade. Moreover, it is not hard to argue that the basis of Jesus' preponderant influence has been his crucifixion and resurrection. Right there, in his passover, western humanism has found its profundity.

Toward the end of his epochal work *Insight,* Bernard Lonergan implies that dogmatic theology can provide the deepest explanation of facts, realities, lives that apparently pay Christian faith no heed or debt.[5] This musing betrays the hopes of the Christian theologian and believer, which are that divine revelation can gain intelligible form and illumine daily affairs. So, for example, theologians, and others, can find that quite traditional dogmatic theses about sin and grace provide the most profound perspectives on politics or the marketplace. Similarly, artists can find that the iconography of Christ crucified furnishes a way of handling human torment not available anywhere else. The transformations that occur when unbelievers are forced to admit the power of symbols of faith are striking. Naturally, the interpretations at work run in two directions, as faith is translated into humanistic terms and humanistic experience is asked to expand its sense of the possible. At the least, however, it becomes plausible that one has to believe in order to understand. At the least, the dogmatic interpretation of human experience as such—what any man or woman might suffer or hope—becomes respectable.

That is what we are asking for Christian approaches to the experience of non-Christians, and what we should be willing to grant, *mutatis mutandis,* to Buddhist or Muslim or other approaches. Truly acute faith has to confess that what it perceives and treasures is universally valid. It cannot accept the understanding of "live and let live" that would make the suffering and joy, the potential and need, of other people off-limits —not to be touched, probed, interpreted in light of the nearly incredible good news that fires its own heart. Certainly the missionary ventures of the western nations have shown how the instinct to share one's good news, the interpretations of the universal human condition that one finds so compelling, can become adulterated or get off the track. Certainly colonialism is the bastardization of proper evangelization. But vibrant faith is bound to carry a missionary imperative, so the great challenge is to make faith sophisticated, fully mature, as well as vibrant. For Christian participants in interreligious dialogue, this challenge might stimulate the ability to articulate the interpretation of universal human experience that they find most compelling without either imposing this interpretation on others or losing the ability to hear the alternate interpretations that others put forth.

The Identity of the Johannine Jesus

The universalism proposed by ancient Christian faith reached a peak in the Johannine christology. The gospel of John is the most explicit of the four in interpreting Jesus as fully divine. When Jesus says, "I am" (a refrain of John's gospel), the allusion to the speech of the Lord to Moses at the burning bush (Ex 3:14) is plain. The Johannine Christ is one with the Father, in such wise that just as the Father always has been, so Jesus always has been. The identity of Jesus reposes in the depths of the Logos. Before Abraham came to be, the Logos enfleshed in Jesus was.

The author of John makes it clear that Jesus' opponents understand his claim and reject it. To their mind, such a claim can only be blasphemous. They think they know who Jesus is, where he comes from, and what he is worth. They cannot conceive that he could be the anointed one of God, the messiah, let alone the Son of God in a literal, ontological sense. The Johannine Jesus understands their difficulties, perhaps even sympathizes with them. But he points to the evidence supporting his claims. If they will not take his word, let them take the testimony of their own senses, which report to them the works he has performed. In their midst, quite publicly, he has given sight to the man born blind, turned the water into wine, cured the paralytic, multiplied the loaves and fishes, raised Lazarus from the dead, and much more. His teaching ought to convince them that he has come from God, but if they will not accept his teaching, let them at least accept his deeds.

The gospel of John is laced with irony, as the dialectic between unbelief and belief plays itself out. The opponents of Jesus are sure they can categorize him, put him in his place, yet the more boldly they pontificate about him, the more they show themselves completely ignorant of Jesus' true nature, and the true nature of the spiritual life. Almost bitterly, the author of John displays the antagonism, the bad will, the murderous determination not to be changed that keeps the antagonists of Jesus from admitting what should be obvious. There was nothing more that Jesus could have done to convince those who finally rejected him and desired his death. They had to choose, for him or against, and they chose against, closing themselves to the light that could have brought them healing and joy.

The interpretation of Jesus put forward in the gospel of John is prejudicial. The author writes from a passionate commitment to Jesus that makes those who opposed Jesus vile. If Jesus, the Word become flesh, represents in the world the divine love, life, and light, the opponents of Jesus represent the contrary: hatred, death, and darkness. If Jesus is the Son of God, the opponents of Jesus are children of Satan, who was a liar from the beginning. The fate of Jesus, crucifixion as the way to glory, has blazed itself into the soul of the author of John. Those responsible for the fate of Jesus, like those opposed to the community of Jesus' followers, have to be on the side of the antiChrist.

The passion, if not counter-hatred, displayed in the gospel of John has created numerous problems. Historically, many Christians thought this gospel licensed hatred of Jews, whom they chose to stigmatize as Christ-killers. Inasmuch as the numerous pogroms of European history, and many other atrocities, depended on such hatred, the gospel of John can seem an unfortunate creation. One can say that common sense, as well as ordinary virtue, ought to have enabled Christians to distinguish between the opponents of the historical Jesus and later Jews, and not to have turned any of the gospels into a basis for antisemitism. The fact remains, however, that Christians did abuse the gospels, perhaps especially the gospel of John, so nowadays responsible theologians point out the potential dangers in the Johannine christology.

Perhaps even more germane to interreligious dialogue, however, is a sympathetic interpretation of the difficulty any of his contemporaries could have had with Jesus' claims. Because of its traditional understanding of God, who could only be One, and its traditional veneration for the torah, God's instruction for Israel, the Judaism of Jesus' day was bound to be skeptical of bold claims to innovative authority. Whether or not the historical Jesus himself made the claims presented in the gospel of John, in all likelihood he did teach with a bold authority and did offer radically new interpretations of the torah. The claims presented in the gospel of John, as noted, make him strictly divine. In the synoptic gospels, Jesus is more circumspect, if not indeed mysterious about his identity (especially in Mark). Yet in all four of the gospels he teaches with authority, not hesitating to contradict legalistic interpretations of the torah or oppose the religious leaders of his day. And whereas some present-day scholars think that most elements of Jesus' teaching were available from other rabbis of his time, there is no doubt that Jesus was the only figure who put together the radically new package represented by the sermon on the mount, the beatitudes, the distillation of the torah to the twofold commandment of love, the teaching about the inexhaustible forgiveness of God, and such parables as the prodigal son and the good Samaritan. In each of the evangelical theologies, as well as in the theology of Paul, Jesus supplants traditional religious authority. In each, he is the bringer of eschatological salvation —the definitive prophet announcing the reign of God.

The problems Jesus presented to his contemporaries only intensified when, after his crucifixion and resurrection, the early Christians began to worship him. Then it was clear, as the gospel of John also showed, that a new interpretation of Israelite monotheism was being offered. Those who found the old interpretation perfectly satisfactory rejected Jesus, Christianity, and such Christian teachings as the Trinity and the eucharist. Could their interpretation of Jesus have been correct?

One of the gains of recent interreligious dialogue has been the creation of the good will necessary to ask such a question dispassionately. If we are to be consistent with what we said about the need to interpret all phenomena in terms of one's own deepest faith convictions, we have to allow non-Christians to make of Christ the best sense they can. If we are to claim that Christian dogma can provide the most profound interpretation of political, artistic, or other perhaps apparently alien data, we have to grant the legitimacy of the Jewish, Buddhist, Muslim, or other non-Christian parallels. Indeed, if we are wise we will listen carefully to the problems that a high christology raises, realizing that we can learn a great deal. At the end, assuming that our Christian commitment has remained unbroken, we may appreciate much better the audacity of such claims as those made for Jesus in the gospel of John. Having been instructed in how awesome true divinity is to the mind of the radical monotheist, the Jew or Muslim passionately confessing that God can only be One, we can appreciate better the power of the conviction that moved the early Christians, many of whom began their religious lives as devoted Jews, to correlate Jesus and the sovereign Lord as Son and Father. Jesus must have conveyed to such early Christians precisely what Paul proclaimed he had: the power and wisdom of God (1 Cor 1:24). By his life, death, and resurrection, he must have become a mystery so rich that he seemed to match the unsearchable riches of the creator and Lord himself. What Jews thought could not be (an enfleshment of divinity), the followers of Jesus thought had happened in Christ. For the followers of Jesus, the mystery of God had not diminished at all. Rather, it had gained a perfect icon, who merely multiplied its wonder, beauty, and incomprehensibility.

Nirvana and Justice

We have suggested some of the difficulty that the radical monotheist can have with the Johannine Christ. We might go on to suggest ways in which Jesus himself was a radical monotheist, deriving his freedom to criticize contemporary religious practices from his immediate sense of the supremacy of the unmasterable Lord. Even the torah, for all its venerability and necessity, could not substitute for the unmasterable Lord. Thus Jesus taught that the sabbath was made for human beings, in their need of the divine mercy. Human beings were not made for the sabbath, in the sense of having to follow slavishly any supposed codifications of the divine will. Jesus himself therefore can emerge as an iconoclast, inasmuch as he preferred the will of his Father, communicated to him directly in the Spirit, to anything merely customary or of human manufacture.

We may bracket the further things one would have to say about christology, if one wanted to dot all the i's and correlate this iconoclasm on the part of the man Jesus with the Christian conviction that he was himself the icon of God. Sufficient for the present moment is the extension of the profoundly religious instinct to abhor idolatry to such eastern creations as the doctrine of nirvana central to Buddhism. As we noted when enumerating three general categories of arguments against the uniqueness of Christ, in addition to historicist arguments there are arguments from the religions' widespread opposition to idolatry and from the historical influence of christology on great injustices perpetrated by western nations. In this section we reflect on these additional arguments, discovering that they can be turned to good account by those wanting to appreciate how radical the original Christian understandings of Jesus were.

For example, the Buddhist teachings about nirvana agree with the instincts of most radical monotheists that one cannot represent ultimate reality. The Buddha tried to avoid metaphysical discussions, thinking that normally they missed the point. The point was to remove the roots of suffering, which lay in desire and ignorance. When one had removed the roots of suffering, the light would dawn and freedom would well up spontaneously. Only then would one be able to understand such doctrines as that explaining nirvana, because only then would one have the experience on which solid doctrine depends. Further, only then would one know, virtually automatically, the limits to which any doctrinal statement is liable, especially doctrinal statements bearing on the Absolute.

The Absolute is that which escapes the conditions, the relativizing factors, characterizing all finite beings. It is easier to describe the Absolute negatively than positively. Negatively, the Absolute is the absence of pain, ignorance, contingency, and the "emptiness" one finds in all limited beings. No limited being explains itself or furnishes its own reason to be. Buddhism rejects the Hindu sense that the Absolute is an independent ground, a necessary being that holds all contingent beings in existence. But it also accepts the intuition of many religious people, western as well as eastern, that reality is greater than the realm normally accredited by human beings. It accepts the idea of transcendence: a beyond found in the midst of ordinary reality yet stretching farther than human beings can comprehend.

The sacredness that Buddhists associate with nirvana, and their instinct that it is not merely the negation of the attributes one associates with finite things, make nirvana comparable to the heaven that western religious thought considers to be the abode of God. One cannot comprehend, measure, or imagine this abode of God. One cannot bring to mind the eternity or infinity (transcendence of time and space) it seems to entail. But one can point to experiences of its presence, times when the human spirit knew that a Beginning and Beyond constituted the very horizon of human knowing and loving.

The mystery so constituting the horizon of human knowing and loving is what Christians believe declared itself definitively in Jesus Christ. Here the word "definitively" begs clarification, so let us note that it means "sufficiently" as well as "once and for all." The declaration of the divine ultimate reality in Jesus Christ was once, singular: no other declaration or revelation took precisely this form or (for Christian faith) was so profound or vivifying. The declaration also was for all people: what God offered in Christ was not limited to Jews or Greeks, because it bore on the core of the human condition, the human nature, found everywhere. The note added by "sufficiently" is that Jesus Christ provides human beings an adequate icon of divinity. In him is available all that anyone needs to be saved and divinized. The ultimate explanation for all of these claims, Christian theologians soon realized, was the literal divinity of Christ. To be all that he was and do all that he had done, Jesus had to have been the Son of God in a strict sense. He could not have been merely adopted, or favored, or used by God, in ways making the term "Son of God" merely honorific. He had to have been divine, the enfleshment of the Logos.

If we translate this into language for Buddhist-Christian dialogue, the result is a Christian hypothesis that Jesus was the human form of the transcendent holiness that Buddhists associate with nirvana. How Jesus then relates to the Buddha (who is the obvious candidate for such a role on Buddhist terms) is a challenging question, best left to the few people thoroughly versed in both christology and buddhology. Expert Buddhists may well reject our hypothetical symmetry, perhaps arguing that Gautama was not such an iconic form, such an incarnation. The question of how devotional Buddhism has regarded the Buddha would remain, since many of the praises of the Buddha and much of the iconography one finds in Buddhist temples leave the impression that the Buddha has been the great metaphor or symbolic form through which the Buddhist masses have approached ultimate reality. Once again, however, any Christian party to discussion of the respective roles of Jesus and the Buddha regarding the revelatory manifestations of the Holy would have to be ready to be corrected by Buddhist insiders.

What seems less problematic, though not problem-free, is the parallel between the Buddhist stipulation of ethical imperatives (*sila*) and the Christian stipulation of a radical moral code. In both systems, for example, justice is the hallmark of authentic religious practice. Buddhism seeks a meditational and sapiential practice that will issue in a lofty morality. The basic precepts of not killing, not lying, not stealing, not committing unchastity, and not taking intoxicants ideally stabilize a practice leading to the greatest selflessness and compassion for other human beings. The Christian commandment to love God with one's whole mind, heart, soul, and strength is partnered with the command to love one's neighbor as oneself. If the first Christian commandment requires worship, the second requires the most radical justice imaginable: treating other people as one's complete equals. Buddhists and Christians no doubt differ in many of their instincts about how to reform society and promote the good life that human beings may aspire to enjoy. At first blush, Christianity seems considerably more inclined to try to change environmental conditions, considerably more political and worldly. This impression may break down as one becomes more familiar with Buddhist history in lands such as China, Tibet, and Japan. What remains, however, is a conviction familiar from Christian spirituality: people will never transform the world and make it worthy of the vision bequeathed by great religious founders such as Jesus and the

Buddha unless they become connected to the beyond (nirvana, the Father) from which the founders drew their strength, wisdom, and creativity.

Jesus and Liberation

The term "founders" has some difficulties. One can say that Jesus and the Buddha gathered disciples, but how formally, institutionally, they envisioned ongoing communities living by their teaching is hard to say. Those who stress the eschatological character of Jesus' preaching and sense of his mission downplay his provision for institutions—his desire to establish a "religion." Those who stress the Jewishness of Jesus' own faith downplay the notion that he sought a radical break with contemporary Judaism, or perhaps even the notion that he sought a radical innovation. Others find data to suggest that Jesus self-consciously selected "the twelve" as a council symbolizing a new Israel, and that Jesus considered the kingdom of God to be as much discontinuous with contemporary Judaism as continuous with it. Finally, all of these and the other questions that the issue of "founding" Christianity entails are bedeviled by the state of the sources. Everything in the New Testament reflects at least a generation's worth of Christian practice and so already is quite interpretational.

The sources relevant to the Buddha's foundation of Buddhism are at least as problematic as those relevant to the foundation of Christianity. Disputes attend such fundamental questions as the Buddha's willingness or reluctance to admit women into the *Sangha,* the monastic community at the center of the Buddhist enterprise. Many Buddhist groups have downplayed the significance of the historical Buddha for Buddhist practice, arguing that Gautama stressed self-reliance and pointed away from himself to the sources of enlightenment available if one followed the Noble Eightfold Path. One would have to advance case by case with Muhammad, Moses, Confucius, and the other figures who come to mind as the most likely candidates for the title "founder" of other religions, and in each such case questions of definition would bulk large. All religions develop across time, and those who keep them in existence (reformers, renovators) may be as significant as those who launched them originally. Most religions have looked to a founding figure as an original source of inspiration, and as a model of the "way" that the religion lays out, but the religions vary greatly in the stress they place on imitating this model. Confucius, the Buddha, Muhammad, and Jesus are all potent exemplars, yet only Jesus is unambiguously considered divinity-in-human form. (We pass over the complex question of the historicity of Krishna, tending to consider him more mythical than the other four exemplars we have mentioned.)

What all of these figures began is less obscure than the intentions with which they began. All began what proved to be ways of finding order, liberation, peace. All could be called, with more or less adaptation, the source of a pathway to salvation: deep healing and reform. What was unique about the way that Jesus launched the deep healing and reform he inaugurated? Among the obvious features, the debts of Christianity to Judaism stand out. Among the subtle features we are most intrigued by what we have been calling iconography or sacramentality.

The debts of Jesus and Christianity to Judaism were massive. Jesus was thoroughly Jewish, and there is little to indicate that he imbibed much of Hellenistic culture, though Hellenistic culture was pervasive in the Judea of his day. Jesus' ideas of God, the law, human nature, justice, human community, and the like all derived from his Jewish upbringing. He fit, and did not fit, such Jewish types as the prophet, the teacher, the wandering holy man. His followers immediately associated him with the messiah that contemporary Judaism was awaiting eagerly. He became embroiled in the burning contemporary issue of how to relate to the Romans ruling the Judea of his day. The teachings of leading rabbis such as Hillel and Shammai may have shaped Jesus' views. When Jesus broke with prevailing tradition, as, for example, in relativizing the torah, he probably sought reform rather than the inauguration of a new, antagonistic pathway. When he claimed authority that, after his death and resurrection, his followers quickly considered divine, he probably was pointing more to God, his Father, than to a divine status of his own clearly manifest to him.

Does this mean that the stronger claims made for Jesus by the New Testament, which already take his followers a considerable distance from what was considered acceptable Judaism, were illegitimate? By no means. The death and resurrection of Jesus revealed more than his ministry could have, and it was inevitable that his followers would reinterpret his significance in the light of his resurrection. After the resurrection, when they were worshiping Jesus as the risen Lord, powerful in their midst as the head of their community, the early Christians were bound to think that from the beginning Jesus had been the Son of God in a strong sense. If his manifestation of the implications of his message and person had been progressive, that was also inevitable. He could not communicate more than his hearers were ready to understand. He himself had to grow in wisdom and grace, since he was fully human. The debts that early Christianity owed to Judaism therefore shrunk somewhat, when it became clear that Jesus was the decisive event not simply of Jewish history but of the history of all humankind. The struggles one can see in the letters of Paul amount to a tremendous effort to clarify what was old in the Christ-event and what was new.

As this effort came to fruition, Jesus was perceived to have liberated humanity from everything that had been oppressing it, including the limitations of the torah. The torah had been ethnically Jewish: limited to the children of Abraham, not incumbent on Gentiles. The torah had been preparatory: a pedagogue for the age prior to the establishment of God's reign, the age of resurrection and the gift of the Spirit making believers cry "Abba, Father." A new freedom blew in the movements of the Spirit. A new stress on love and communing with a God offering divine life came to the fore.

In these and other ways, the early Christians established a typology that made Judaism the *ante* and Christianity the *post*. Jesus was the dividing line, the threshold. Jesus had fulfilled Jewish prophecy, the books of which became part of an "old" testament. What Israel had looked forward to, as the fulfillment of divine promises, implicit or explicit, associated with the covenants (Abrahamic, Mosaic, Davidic), Jesus had brought—and then some. To the Christian mind, Jesus elevated such promises to a new level, providing a grander fulfillment than the old prophets had intuited: divine sonship and daughterhood, eternal life.

When we consider this entire complex of notions bearing on the Christian sense of the liberation movement that Jesus launched, the iconic character that Jesus assumed becomes dazzling. Meeting Hellenistic (non-Jewish) hopes and ideals as well as Jewish ones, the sacramental Christ came to center an immensely powerful conviction that liberation had occurred, the eschaton had been realized, the gulf between divinity and humanity had been bridged. Jesus had saved people from sin, brought heaven to earth, incarnated divinity, mediated divine wisdom and life, displayed the love for which all human hearts were longing, and provided the essentials of a human community befitting the new age he had created. In the Spirit of Jesus, and with the guidance of his parables, other teachings, works of healing, and the like, human beings could relate to one another as members of a single great, holy, Christic "body." They could think that they shared a common life, as though they were all branches of a Christic vine. And they could renew their convictions, recall the great deeds that had saved them, experience again the movements of divine love by worshiping the Christ present in their midst, by praying to the Father through Christ and in the Spirit. So Jesus, divine and human, historical and re-surrected, teacher and lover, healer and God, food and promise, sup-plied all that the Christian community could need. In every substantial way, he liberated believers from the dead-ends that had haunted them, from the partialities that had discouraged them. What he founded was a new vision, a new community, a new being, all of them divine and human, theandric, just as he was. What he was icon of was nothing less than God's mystery—God's plan for human beings, which came into time from the recesses of eternity in the Word made flesh. No wonder his followers have considered Jesus to be unique, sufficient, and unsur-passable. No wonder they have insisted that the most fundamental stratum of any person's salvation passes through Jesus the Christ.

The Temper of the Unitive Spirit

This fundamental stratum of any person's salvation rivets the at-tention of the Christian of unitive temper. If the Christian pluralist is happy enough to shift from a Christocentric to a theocentric view of salvation and arrange Jesus alongside a variety of other saviors, the Christian of unitive temper is happy to consider what Jesus accom-plished to be the pith of salvation wherever salvation is found.

This unitive Christian does not have to subscribe without qualifica-tion to the teachings of Cyprian, Augustine, and some of the church councils that outside the Catholic Church there is no salvation. What church membership can mean in this context of the contours of salva-tion is rightfully a matter of vigorous debate. But the unitive Christian's instinct is that what God revealed and accomplished through the God-man Jesus Christ is the axial line of human salvation. There, as nowhere else, the divine love offering humanity its most radical healing and fulfillment stands sacramentalized, enfleshed, put into the iconic form that we incarnate spirits require. There the grace that explodes the limitations humanity tends to place on human potential stands fully humanized. Bloodied, yet so beautiful as to prove to the believer that the Christian way is surpassingly fitting, Jesus stands forth as a unique everyman. He bears the afflictions of all the broken men and women who have ever suffered. He fulfills the hopes, the barely glimpsed visions, of all the poets and dreamers, the mystics and sages, who have seen what humanity might be and felt humanity's aptness for divinity.

The question of how what happened in and through Jesus relates to people outside the history of Christian cultures remains a difficult one. As long as we try to find a strictly historical relationship, or to imagine something linear strung out from heaven, we are not likely to find a satisfactory expression for our instinct that Jesus is the best, the only adequate, everyman and savior. We do better when we analyze the basic requirements of salvation and ponder the solidarity of all human beings in such requirements. Whether or not all human beings have originated from the same protohuman stock, all human beings—animals with reflective consciousness—have been aware of divine mystery, human suffering, and human longing for a fulfillment that space and time never provide in stable fashion. Inasmuch as Jesus solved the comprehensive problem implied in these universal human needs (or any others one might nominate: triumph over death, victory over evil, desire to see the source of the world's meaning face to face, and so forth), Jesus was the absolute bringer of salvation, the universal success.

Does this mean that humanity has not had other saviors? No, of course not. The Buddha, Confucius, Krishna, and many others have healed broken spirits, inspired noble lives. Does it mean that no other historical figure has been so profound, adequate, central, universal—such an everyman, so obviously a universal savior? For Christian conviction, yes. For Buddhist, Confucian, Hindu, or other convictions, not necessarily (in fact, probably no). What would happen in a detached discussion of the merits of the different candidates for the title of universal savior, and whether such a discussion would be profitable, are debatable questions. No one with any experience of interreligious debate should expect a clear consensus that Jesus, or any other soteriological figure, would emerge as obviously the absolute bringer of salvation. But in this book we are not working on the basis of comparative religious studies, even if we think that Jesus would fare exceedingly well, were the criteria for the universal savior expressed as they ought to be. In fact, we are not interested in any competition between Jesus and other soteriological figures, even when it may seem that discussing the adequacy, the comprehensiveness, of Jesus' accomplishment makes such competition inevitable.

Our interest is the match between what full, Catholic Christian faith finds in Jesus and the needs that human beings display always and everywhere. Our interest is grace and sin, divine life and death, revelation and ignorance, love and the human spirit's deepest yearnings. For all the fleshly needs of human beings, there is Jesus the complete human being, the tender yet powerful healer, the bread of life, the teacher of righteousness, the winsome leader. For all the spiritual needs of human beings, there is Jesus the icon of divine mystery, the forgiver of sins, the resurrected Lord, the abider in believers' hearts, the sender of the Spirit, the incarnation of divine wisdom. This exact junction of flesh and spirit, of the human and the divine, of the mortal and the immortal, of sacramentality and inexhaustible mystery satisfies our sense of what salvation entails. Indeed, it far exceeds what we would consider sufficient help to merit the designation "salvation." What the Buddha, Muhammad, Confucius, Socrates, and many others have seen and accomplished amounts, in our view, to a significant salvation. But in no case other than Jesus do we find salvation displayed so comprehensively, humanly, and transcendently (stretching so far forward into the endless mystery of God).

Consider simply one aspect of the Christian iconography for such salvation: the eucharist. To what we are calling the unitive mind, the eucharist gathers together the essentials of any person's soteriological requirements. The basic symbolism is of food, feeding, nourishment. Christ is bread and wine, body and blood, that sustains the full person, body and soul, in divine life. Those who eat the flesh of Christ and drink his blood will live forever—because the life nourished in them is God's own life. By eating this flesh and drinking this blood, the believer abides in the life of Father, Son, and Spirit, than which there is nothing more ultimate, desirable, profound, or fulfilling. Moreover, the eucharist conveys forgiveness of sins. It builds up the community of believers. It recalls the passover of Christ, from death to resurrection and ascension to the Father's right hand. The sacrifice of Christ, his pouring out his life for his friends, comes into mind at each eucharistic celebration. The present lordship of Christ comes to mind: he is in the midst of his community, his body, as one who leads them on their pilgrimage, who has gone before them and comes from across the great divide. The Christian eucharist is the great *anamnesis,* the great memorial, recall, representation of the incarnational mysteries. Through word (the biblical reminder of Jesus' teaching and work) and sacrament (iconic modes of communion with Jesus, the Father, the Spirit, and the saints), the Christian community resets the basic lines of reality, reaffirms its fundamental faith, hope, and love. Because human beings are weak, forgetful, superficial, and so many other impedimental things, they need regular, ideally daily reminders about the iconic mystery in which they live, move, and have their being. Because human beings are embodied spirits, they need visible, audible, palpable ways of appropriating the salvation—the healing and elevating—lavished upon them in Christ. Because they constantly doubt the divine love, human beings need almost excessive displays of how far God was willing to go on their behalf. All of this the eucharist furnishes, convincing the unitive Christian that Christ is the absolute, the nonpareil bringer of salvation.

Jesus and Suffering

If we wish to contemplate what salvation is from, several words come to mind. "Suffering" certainly is one word, and "sin" can rightly be another. In this section we deal with suffering. The salvation that Jesus accomplished bore intimately on suffering, as his hanging from the cross shows. Surely he bore our frailties and afflictions, fulfilling the typology of Second Isaiah's suffering servant. He was bruised for our iniquities. In his sufferings human beings have been able to realize the inhumanity to one another that their kind has perpetrated regularly throughout history.

Jesus suffered innocently. He had done no wrong meriting the arrest, beating, mockery, and crucifixion imposed on him. Arguments that the Romans were right to fear a political uprising, or that the Jewish opponents of Jesus were right to fear a religious revolution, miss the mark. For Christian interpretation, Pontius Pilate, the representative of Rome, himself avowed the innocence of Jesus, even as he illogically, cowardly, allowed Jesus to be mistreated. For Christian interpretation, the high priest and the Pharisees deeply opposed to Jesus thought it better that one man die than that the status quo be upset. The great crime that Jesus committed, the actual reason that he was killed the way notorious criminals were, was that he forced people to face the living God. Unless people were willing to be turned around, be converted, they tended to consider Jesus their enemy. He asked them for things they were unwilling to give: complete honesty, confession of sin, willingness to make a new start, willingness to try to trust God completely and love their neighbors as they loved themselves. Those who responded to this challenge positively found peace and joy. Those who rejected the challenge resented Jesus' having asked them for more than they could muster. According to the gospels, many who rejected Jesus' challenge even came to hate him and desire his death.

The association between Jesus' sufferings and the salvation that he accomplished is most intimate and has to be pondered carefully if one is to appreciate the deep cuts of the Christian good news. As well, this association seems to be unique, something that the other soteriological figures whom comparativists tend to range alongside Jesus did not establish. The Buddha did not die like a criminal, linking his analysis of how to overcome suffering with a sundering death, in complete disgrace and rejection, that made it clear he himself had drunk the cup of suffering to its dregs. Socrates did die for his principles, but quite peacefully, in full dignity, and by his own hand. Only Jesus had no comeliness in his death, nothing noble, dignified, heroic. Only Jesus brought divinity to bear on human suffering so intimately that orthodox theologians, basing their predication on the unity of the God-man, felt they could say, "God died on the cross." In Jesus' death on the cross, the possibility opened that divinity itself could suffer, go into abandonment, undergo the wrenching wrought by defeat and death. How one could square this possibility with the self-sufficiency of God has never been explained adequately. Any such squaring rests in the mysteriousness of God's freedom and love. But those who respect the freedom and love of God have to maintain the possibility that divinity could find ways to share humanity's vulnerability and mortality. Indeed, those who respect the crucifixion of Christ have to maintain the possibility that only crucifixion could express the depth of the horrors from which divinity determined to save humankind, and the depth of the divine love.

Christianity has said that suffering is not the final word about either Jesus or humankind. The good news is not only that God was willing to suffer with human beings but also that God's suffering defeated humanity's greatest enemies. Easter is the consummate Christian feast, because Easter celebrates God's resurrection of human life from suffering, sin, death, and all the other predators that have slashed at human beings since the rise of the human race. In Easter, Christians have seen the fulfillment of the potential hinted in the exodus, the return from the exile, and the other great events of Israelite history. They have considered the sufferings of Jesus the fulfillment of the Israelite Lord's willingness to sojourn with his people and share their exiles, and they have considered the resurrection of Jesus the fulfillment of the establishment of the chosen people in the promised land, in the city of David, in the eschatological kingdom.

Suffering is universal. The Buddha proclaimed this truth, and common observation verifies it. If Jesus overcame suffering, broke its back or tore out its roots, then Jesus was and is the universal savior. The resurrection is the great symbol of Christian faith that Jesus did precisely that. Since the resurrection, the Christian proposal has been that if people commit themselves to Christ, the victory of Christ symbolized in the resurrection can become people's own. Believers can pass beyond the clutches of death and suffering, in the sense that death and suffering will not be the last words. The last words will be life and beatitude. Where death and suffering abounded, life and beatitude will abound the more—will abound eternally.

But if Jesus has overcome suffering and death, why is our world still rife with them? What can it possibly mean to proclaim the definitive victory of Christ when so many of his followers, both confessed and anonymous, repeat his march to Calvary, die in shame or agony? It can possibly mean that divine wisdom thinks it necessary for the followers of Jesus, confessed or anonymous, to take up their crosses and repeat his passover. It can possibly mean that there is no cheap grace, no union with Christ or reception of salvation that is merely extrinsic or imputed. Grace and salvation have to get as deeply into our marrow as suffering and death have. The divine genius is to have made suffering and death the most constant, basic means by which grace and salvation penetrate human beings. If one uses Christ as one's interpretational key, humanity only comes into its own through suffering and death. The things that seem humanity's greatest curse turn out to serve humanity's and God's good purposes.

But isn't this to say that God is perverse, a sadistic savior? Couldn't

God have found a nicer, easier, happier way to solve humanity's problems and communicate divine life? Who knows? Speculatively, there may be dozens of ways that divinity could have taken us human beings to itself and wiped every tear from our eyes. In the actual world order that we inhabit, however, God has chosen to use our suffering and death. Paradoxically, God has chosen to suffer our suffering and die our death as the way to assure our fulfillment and immortality. We can believe this or not, depending on our willingness or unwillingness to commit ourselves to Jesus. What we cannot do is commit ourselves to Christ and believe that salvation occurs otherwise than by God's embrace of human suffering and death.

So the world is saved in the measure that it believes, explicitly or implicitly, that the suffering, death, and resurrection of Christ have brought human nature into God's hands, into God's life. The sufferings that human beings continue to endure remind Christians of nothing less than Jesus' way of the cross. When human hope rises about such sufferings, Christians find reminders and anticipations of the resurrection. When people seem to despair, to be unable to imagine a reality beyond suffering and richer than it, Christians have to hope and pray for them, asking God, in the divine mercy that must already be soliciting such people's hearts, must already be whispering encouragement and hope, to see them through.

Jesus and Forgiveness

The second word we consider in this pursuit of discovering what salvation is from is "sin." Jesus communicates radical healing to people by mediating God's forgiveness of their sins. What is sin? It is missing the mark, in the sense of flying by the target set one by one's humanity. It is disobeying the divine will, as Adam and Eve did in the garden, where they learned about nakedness and shame. It is acting irrationally, against one's own good and the good of the whole community. And, above all, it is refusing to love the basic conditions of one's life: the mysteriousness of one's divine origins and spiritual milieu; the necessity that one die and hope for an immortal meaning; the necessity that one cooperate with other people, help them, love them, count them flesh of one's flesh and bone of one's bone.

We all sin by failing to hit the mark, by disobeying the call of God in conscience, by acting irrationally, and by refusing to love. We all feel twisted, soiled, tempted to despair, because our sin means there is little health in us, means we are condemned to existential frustration and having to fear God. We do not have the easy relationship with God that Jesus did, because we are not sinless as Jesus was. We do not have the open relationship with nature that Jesus did, because we want things from nature that are not right, that gratify our egocentricity and lust more than they cooperate with the harmony of creation. We suffer in our human relationships, both as individuals and as nations, because we will not love other people the way we love ourselves but insist on trying to take advantage of others.

Sin produces the majority of suffering in our world. Certainly, flood, famine, earthquake, cancer, heart disease, senility, and a dozen other natural evils cause immense suffering. But most people are hungry, or feel humiliated, or fear their lives have no worth because of human sin. Nature can produce enough food, shelter, and beauty to satisfy five billion human beings, along with myriad other creatures, if those human beings are willing to live cooperatively. The world religions offer limitless stimuli to great meaning, as do music, art, physical science, social service, education, prayer, and the other humanistic preoccupations. When people love one another, look out for one another, dedicate themselves to educating and healing one another, they do not hesitate to affirm that life is a great gift, a treasure moving them to profound gratitude. The problem is not with the physical universe, or with God, or with Christ. The problem is with ourselves, as individuals and as groups.

We do not know what to do with ourselves. We do not know how to understand ourselves, especially our propensity to sin and foul our nest. The wars, murders, rapes, thefts, lies, and other cruelties that blot the historical record are enigmas. Why human beings should have preferred slaughter to cooperation, destruction to creativity, cruelty to kindness is a great unknown. The fact that Jesus was not spared the effects of sin but saved humanity while suffering as a victim of sin boggles the mind on two counts. First, it brings home how thoroughly human the Logos became. Like the rest of us, Jesus suffered the effects of human malice, learned about pure nastiness, and felt ridiculous. Second, it magnifies the divine compassion. God was willing to embrace not just suffering but also evil. God was willing to let human beings do their worst and outstrip it with love.

How do we experience forgiveness? As the release of a great burden. As the straightening of a bent spirit. As the flood of light into a dark and dank cellar, an interiority we were ashamed to face. As the restoration of peace and love between enemies. Forgiveness says that we can begin anew. It says that God can open what we thought was a dead end. By forgiveness we can be reconciled to our enemies. We can be reconciled to God. We can be reconciled to ourselves. Any of the relationships that we had twisted, abused, thought we had ruined may be restored, if God's grace, God's love, takes it in hand. Seventy times seven (limitlessly), God will help us to our feet, accept the wishes of our better self, recreate our potential to express the divine nature.

Psychologically, forgiveness is precisely the word, the experience, that the self most needs, because the self is most tormented by guilt: feelings that it will always be in the wrong, always be dirty and inadequate. Socially, forgiveness is precisely the word, the experience, that groups most need if they are to break their vicious circles. Catholics and Protestants in Northern Ireland will not forgive one another the centuries of mutual hurting, so they continue to hate and maim. Arabs and Israelis will not move beyond self-serving views of justice, so they never make a radically new start. Women have to forgive men, and men have to forgive women, if we are ever to conquer sexism. Whites and blacks, Asians and Europeans, the old generation and the new generation—all have to experience the possibility of burying the dysfunctional past if they are to believe in a good, common future. Parents and children, spouses at one another's throats, labor and management, wealthy and poor—all the dialectical, antagonistic stand-offs that bring tensions and tears into our world cry out for a reconciliation, a reworking, that depends on forgiveness.

Yet the most profound dimension of forgiveness is vertical. The horizontal operations of forgiveness are crucial for domestic and social order, but the vertical dimension, where God offers us mercy and forgiveness, is the deepest need of our souls. God has never offended us, even though on occasion we may indulge the feeling that God has. Just and true is the Lord, righteous in all his ways. We have no rights before God. There is no constitution spelling out how God has to treat us. We came from nothingness and without God's support we would sink back into nothingness. We have no natural claim on God's life or personal love, no entitlement to revelation or a share in the trinitarian processions. Remember, man, woman, that thou art dust, and unto dust thou shalt return. Remember that when we were sinners, God loved us, creating beauty and being where there was only ugliness and a void. The forgiveness that God gives us is a gratuity piled upon a gratuity. The love God gives us stems from God's own goodness, not goodness we possess independently. If the Lord should count iniquities, who could bear it? If the Lord were not compassionate and merciful, long-suffering and abounding in steadfast love, who could survive?

The fact that Jesus preached a forgiveness of sins, and was so bold as to assure people who approached him in faith that their sins were forgiven, outraged his enemies. It was bad enough that Jesus was breaking the sabbath conventions, healing outside the appointed times. But that he should presume to tell people God was removing their moral debts was infuriating. Indeed, it was blasphemous, for who but God alone can forgive sins?

Precisely, the supporters of Jesus said. Jesus could not have been sane and promised forgiveness of sins had he not been divine. Unless he were speaking for God, he would have been the most sacrilegious of people. But clearly he was not sacrilegious. Clearly he was concerned about nothing so much as his relationship with his Father. So when he cured people's souls, giving them a new start in the moral life, he had to be acting as he thought and felt the Father wanted him to. He had to be telling people that the Father cared more for the love in their hearts than their record on the accountant's books. Tax collectors and prostitutes would go into the kingdom before people who considered themselves righteous, because tax collectors and prostitutes could have more love in their hearts. The woman who wiped Jesus' feet with her hair received forgiveness, not because of her merits but because Jesus saw in her heart a great desire to respond to the divine goodness.

It is the divine goodness that Jesus the forgiver of sins emphasizes. It is the unmerited character of the Father's embrace of the prodigal son that stands out. God forgives human beings, as God saves human beings from death and suffering, because it is God's nature to be that good. The logic ruling God's heart is not a logic of justice. It is a logic of love, a desire that no child of the divine design should be crippled by guilt, that all the people of God should feel the warmth of being restored to the divine bosom. The desire in God's heart is that human beings become fully alive. Becoming fully alive requires sloughing off one's guilt, standing erect because one's conscience has been cleared and one can look God in the eye.

As the classical Protestant reformers saw, human beings do not accomplish this for themselves. Salvation from sin is wholly God's doing. The work of human beings is to believe in God's goodness and open themselves to God's love. The emphasis Jesus places on the divine desire to forgive human beings may not be unique among the great religious founders, but it is certainly distinctive. Muhammad and the Qur'an speak more about forgetfulness than about sin. Judaism speaks more about justice and law than about forgiveness, though forgiveness is not lacking. For the eastern traditions, the great enemy is not sin but ignorance. Even when one realizes that ignorance and sin are closely tied, the message of Jesus that a God as personal as a parent is eager to give people a new moral start remains distinctive. Nowhere in the world religions does one find a greater emphasis on the goodness of the Lord, a greater sense of the freedom that comes when one receives the Lord's Spirit of forgiveness. Inasmuch as such forgiveness is crucial for the world's mental health, the forgiveness of sins that Jesus proclaimed is another reason to think him the universal savior.

Summary Reflections I: High Christology and Prayer

If we now gather together the implications of the Catholic Christian conviction that Jesus is uniquely saving, what might we conclude about prayer? First, we might conclude that few religions other than Christianity make their mainstream prayer, their common liturgy, an address to their founder. Muslims pray to Allah, not to Muhammad. Jews pray to the Lord, not to Moses. Some Buddhists pray to Gautama, but many do not. Some Confucians have prayed to Confucius, and some Taoists have prayed to Lao Tzu, but whether this has been true worship, implying the identification of Confucius or Lao Tzu with the holiest, most ultimate reality in existence, is doubtful. Hindus worshiping Krishna certainly have prayed to a god-man, but the historicity of Krishna, and so his actual (in contrast to his imaginary) humanity, is suspect. That leaves Jesus standing alone, distinctive for the degree to which his followers have felt that everything connoted by the word "divine," as well as everything connoted by the word "human," applies to him. Neither the Virgin Mary nor the Christian saints share this distinction with Jesus. For orthodox faith (faith responding to the demand that it speak clearly and universally), "Christ our God" has named someone unique.

Second, we might conclude from the uniqueness that a high christology finds in Jesus that all prayer to God can be configured to the patterns set by the incarnation. This is clear when one contemplates sacramental prayer, for the enfleshment of the Logos makes it fitting that prayer should be to the Father, through the Son, and in the Spirit. It is less clear when one contemplates apophatic prayer (prayer that proceeds "negatively," stressing the divine darkness and immensity, rather than any forms, however legitimate). There the realization of the incarnational pattern depends on two insights. The first is that the person praying always remains an incarnate spirit (never becomes disembodied, purely a soul) and so always can be fitted to the pattern of Jesus the Son addressing the Father. The second is that the divine darkness or immensity that negative ways of praying stress is the trinitarian God, whose own internal structures, for us human beings, create the patterns of Jesus' prayer. The God too bright to appear to the human mind as anything but darkness, too simple to appear as anything but mysterious, is the Father expressing the divine being in the Word that has taken flesh, the Word reflecting all that the Father is, and the Spirit circulating the love of the Father and the Son. Even when the human spirit, western or eastern, feels the need to deal with divinity wordlessly, imagelessly, in a cloud of unknowing, Christian faith holds that the divinity being dealt with—adored, waited upon, abided with—is the trinitarian community revealed through the prayer of Jesus.

Third, the prayer of Jesus, along with the rest of his revelation, urges people to move toward God with the confidence and trust of children approaching the best of parents. It urges people to ask for help, for forgiveness, for fulfillment. The image of God published by the prayer and teaching of Jesus makes God far better than what human beings usually assume. The God to whom Jesus prayed always heard him, always loved him, always could be trusted. If Jesus did not understand how God was responding to his prayer, he credited that to his own limitations. To God he credited only goodness, giving his Father a blank check. What could he do better with his life and fate than place them into his Father's keeping? Where would they be more secure? Those who sought to secure their lives by their own efforts were choosing against their own best interests. Any day their lives might be "required" of them. None of them knew the day or place when God would call them to account. So the wise among them would not place their trust in their money, or their possessions, or their reputation, or their friends, or even their own good deeds. The wise among them would place their trust in the goodness of the Lord, the love of the Father.

What does it mean to pray to Christ, or the Father, or the Holy Spirit with evangelical trust? Only the saints can tell us reliably, but one might intuit that it means to make God wholly real—the most real thing in one's inventory. God would then be more secure and reliable than one's family circle, one's agenda for work, one's own body, even one's own mind. Each of those is fragile. Even though we are bound to take them for granted, any of them can be snatched away at a stroke. Spouses die. Children move away. One's work sours. One's body fails. A tiny blood clot can cloud one's mind. Through all of this, the saints suggest, God remains, can be relied upon, keeps "reality" from entering a tailspin.

Prayer to a God believed to be this real must be nearly automatic. It must be more in the mode of acknowledging a permanent presence than in the mode of conducting an occasional interview. What the Bible implies by speaking of God's sojourning with Israel, or of Israel's sojourning with God, connotes some of this permanent mutual presence. What the biblical imagery of the marriage between the Lord and Israel, or between Christ and the church, connotes also is germane. The mystics may reach a state in which they are constantly united with God and aware of the divine presence. For many of them, God is the ground of their spirits, more intimate to them than they are to themselves. They have the gift of finding God in all things. They sense the meaning of God's being "all in all," of Christ's being the universal Lord. In God they live, move, and have their being. God numbers all the hairs of their heads. Not a leaf falls, not a sparrow flies, not a lily flowers without its reminding them of God's support of all creatures in being. So they pray as they breathe, as they eat, as the blood circulates through their veins and arteries. Prayer is natural, because the One to whom they pray is always nigh.

They speak to God intimately, personally, even presumptuously. Reverence remains, but loving familiarity is more prominent. On their model, God is the Father whom one unhesitatingly asks for bread, knowing one will not receive a stone. God is the mother whom one depends upon like a nursing child, never considering the possibility that she could abandon one. When God does seem distant, one blames one's own distractions, inattentions, sins and self-concerns. The distance of God is one's greatest regret, one's sharpest suffering. But at the fine point of one's soul, where one hopes that the Holy Spirit works at the advocacy that Jesus promised he would, one trusts that somehow, someday, all will be well—because of what one believes God to be and who God has been in the past.

The prayer of the saints is a profound love affair. Muslim saints such as Rabi'a and Rumi prove this, as do Hindu saints, Jewish saints, and Christian saints. Many questions remain about the best way to characterize the meditations of easterners who do not stress a personal God, but we may bracket them here. Here our focus is what prayer formed by belief in the full divinity and full humanity of Christ should be like. The upshot of this focus seems to be that it should be like Jesus' own prayer: the basic nourishment of one's being.

Jesus was confident that God knew all his needs, supported all his ministry, regretted all his sufferings, and would see him through whatever crises came upon him. The bond between Jesus and his Father was completely personal (so much so that it gives new resonance to the term "person"). What the Father could expect from him, and what he could expect from the Father, flowed from the history of their communing. They were one—in mind, heart, soul, affection. Jesus had no other reason to be than to serve the Father's will, plan, desire for human beings. His entire goal was to reveal the goodness of the Father, the wonderful news of the Father's nearness, the forgiveness of sins and reordering of all human potential that the Father longed to bestow.

The fact that many human beings rejected the Father's will only intensified Jesus' prayer. The fact that sin abounded only showed him the need for grace to abound the more. Whatever discouragement Jesus felt never overbalanced his confidence that serving his Father was the best (the only) thing he could do. The implication for the prayer of Jesus' followers is clear. They have to try to believe, with Paul, that nothing can separate them from the love of God in Christ Jesus. They have to make the Father the center of their lives and give him, through

Jesus and in the Spirit, a blank check. As they do, they act out the axial Christian belief that Jesus has the words of everlasting life, because Jesus is the absolute bringer of salvation.

Summary Reflections II: High Christology and Social Justice

Just as high christology, stressing the divinity and so sacramental character of the Word made flesh, has supportive implications for Christian prayer, so it has supportive implications for Christian work to advance social justice. The fact that it is the divine Son who emptied himself (Phil 2:5–11) to take flesh gives Christians a model of self-spending that can make work for social justice seem natural. Behind the emptying of the Son is the self-giving of the Father, who gives all that he is to generate the Son. The Son in turn gives all of the divine substance back to the Father, while the result of their mutual self-giving is the Spirit. The entire divine community therefore is constituted by self-giving. The farthest reaches of the Christian doctrine of grace carry the intuition that this self-giving has become the goal of human history. The Father has given the Son into history for the salvation of humankind. The Son and the Father have given the Spirit into history, to guide first Jesus and then those bonded to Jesus in the divine love. If people will abide with Jesus and the Spirit, they will enjoy the Father. The communion of Father, Son, and Spirit will become their own, because the God who supports them in being will be none other than the Trinity. The Trinity might have shown human beings only its external "face," but it has chosen instead to be with and in human beings what it is in itself: a perfect community of love. So the grace that divinizes human beings is the self-giving of the divine persons. In elevating human beings beyond what human beings have any right to expect (in providing deathlessness, eternal joy and peace in adoration of God), the Trinity has made self-giving the new horizon for Christian wisdom.

How does self-giving relate to social justice? Quite directly. When people act as though they are to love their neighbors as themselves, they target the most radical social justice. When the selves people love are partakers of the divine nature, they verge upon the realization that every fellow citizen can be, should be, considered a partaker of the divine nature. If God has offered the divine love everywhere, as the universal fruits of holiness make credible, then everywhere people are dignified by the presence in their hearts and midst of the holy love that Christians associate with the Trinity.

In Africa and Asia, where the prevailing cultures may make language such as this seem foreign, the substance of what this language is saying can still apply. People who do not confess Christ with their lips can be living the divine life that Christ clarified. Similarly, people in Latin America who desperately need food, clothing, education, health care, peace, and fair-sharing can be manifesting the cross of Christ. When any human beings deal with the problems standing in the way of creating a decent life for themselves or other people, they are dealing with sin and the other impediments to sharing on the model of the trinitarian persons. When any human beings find the strength, the insight, the selflessness to advance social justice, they are manifesting the power of Christ's Spirit. Social justice, like simple helpfulness between two unpretentious neighbors, is nothing less than the practical side of the respect any member of the body of Christ owes all other members (actual or potential).

This may sound remote, arcane, esoteric, "theological" in an elitist sense. It is nothing of the kind. Until we have seen that a high christology, making human flesh the focal point of God's self-giving in history, is the most real perspective on human affairs, we have not penetrated Christian faith very deeply. The street person panhandling for a dollar is best understood in light of the iconic Christ. So is the teenage mother living on welfare, the addict come down with AIDS, the child starving in East Africa, the victim of ethnic violence in Azerbaijan, the soldier trying to thwart the drug cartels of Medellín. Victim or oppressor, saint or sinner, any human being comes into clearest focus when viewed through the lens of the iconic Christ. That is a simple translation of Christian faith that Christ is the way, the truth, and the light. For Christians not to accept such practical, political implications of christology is for them to show themselves inconsistent, or unbelieving. The virulence of racism, the evil of insider trading in the stock market, the sacrilege of rape, the heinous character of drug-dealing—all only emerge into their full, three-dimensional reality when one correlates them with the Christ who emptied himself for the sake of his fellow human beings.

Action for social justice is the hallmark of people who have accepted the solidarity of human beings revealed by the incarnation. The church, which gathers together the followers of Christ, ought to be a model of social justice—an exemplar of the social order that the divine love manifested in Christ implies. It is axiomatic that power in the church is for service, so the degree to which members of the church promote themselves rather than the service of others is a touchstone of the church's sinfulness. All the more so, the degree to which secular politics is dominated by power-plays is a touchstone of the corruption of secular politics. When a blind person leads a blind person, both fall into the ditch. When politics, or business, or medicine, or education tries to prescind from the divine self-giving, the divine template for human success, it is bound to go awry.

Nothing is more wearying than the spiritual blindness dominating secular institutions (and all too prevalent in the churches). Because they refuse to tell the truth, to work in the light, to share burdens and rewards equally, human beings twist their relationships and their souls. A few people end up very wealthy while a great many more suffer terrible want. Billions of dollars are wasted on arms, on glitzy communications, on drugs and pornography and other spiritual poisons. Meanwhile, little children go without proper nourishment, physical and spiritual. Old people go without proper care and friendship. Women suffer abuse on several different levels. And everywhere the majority of people are much sadder than God intended. Social justice is any action, any renovation of human relationships, that would right any part of this terrible imbalance. It is speaking up for health rather than perversion, for love rather than lust, for cooperation rather than competition, for peace rather than fighting, bickering, backbiting, stealing, and the dozens of other ways that people deny the basic truth of their human equality.

The sacramental Christ relativizes all pretenses to superiority. Compared to the riches revealed in Christ, human riches, honors, bases for boasting and the like seem utter trash. The Fortune 500, the Social Register, and all the other economic or social indexes of "success" melt like snow before the sun. Vanity of vanities, none of them is worth a penny in the sight of the Lord. The waste (of money, of time, of energy, of ambition) they stimulate shows them to be tools of Satan. Consistently, they support the unjust status quo and oppose the conversions necessary to establish the kingdom of God. Consequently, any measured attack on them serves the kingdom of God. Anything that cuts them down to size and throws them on the refining fire of God's holiness and justice is a good work, worthy of the Christ blazing from the pages of Revelation.[6]

NOTES

1. See Karl Rahner, THEOLOGICAL INVESTIGATIONS, vol. 16 (New York: Seabury, 1979), p. 219.

2. See Paul F. Knitter, "Hans Küng's Theological Rubicon," and Hans Küng, "What Is True Religion? Toward an Ecumenical Criteriology," in TOWARD A UNIVERSAL THEOLOGY OF RELIGION, ed. Leonard Swidler (Maryknoll, N.Y.: Orbis, 1987), pp. 224–230 and 231–250.

3. See Stanley S. Harakas, "Orthodox Christianity and Theologizing," in TOWARD A UNIVERSAL THEOLOGY OF RELIGION, pp. 73–78.

4. See Aloysius Pieris, S.J., "East in the West: Resolving a Spiritual Crisis," HORIZONS, 15/2 (Fall 1988), 337–346.

5. See Bernard J. F. Lonergan, S.J., INSIGHT: A STUDY OF HUMAN UNDERSTANDING (New York: Philosophical Library, 1958), pp. 731–748.

6. Our own christology has been most formed by such Catholic theologians as Karl Rahner, Bernard Lonergan, Edward Schillebeeckx, Hans Küng, and Hans Urs von Balthasar. See, for example, Karl Rahner, FOUNDATIONS OF CHRISTIAN FAITH (New York: Seabury, 1978); Karl Rahner and Wilhelm Thüsing, A NEW CHRISTOLOGY (New York: Seabury, 1980); Bernard Lonergan, DE VERBO INCARNATO (Rome: Gregorian University Press, 1964); Bernard Lonergan, DE CONSTITUTIONE CHRISTI ONTOLOGICA ET PSYCHOLOGICA (Rome: Gregorian University Press, 1964); Bernard Lonergan, DE DEO TRINO, 2 vols. (Rome: Gregorian University Press, 1964); Edward Schillebeeckx, JESUS (New York: Seabury, 1979); Edward Schillebeeck, CHRIST (New York: Seabury, 1980); Hans Küng, ON BEING A CHRISTIAN (Garden City, N.Y.: Doubleday, 1976); Hans Urs von Balthasar, THE VON BALTHASAR READER, eds. Medard Kenland and Werner Loser (New York: Crossroad, 1985). For an interesting comparison between the analogy of being on which Roman Catholic christology has tended to depend and the analogy of faith used by the premier Protestant theologian Karl Barth, see THE VON BALTHASAR READER, pp. 23–24.

Chapter 5

Limitation, Uniqueness, and Catholic Spirituality

Defenses Against Historicism

We have seen some of the arguments against the traditional Christian view that Jesus Christ is the unique savior of humankind, and also some of the arguments for this traditional view. In this final chapter we attempt an application of our ruminations to Catholic Christian spirituality. How should a balanced view of Christ's uniqueness shape Christian prayer, Christian social action, Christian thought and imagery about the relationships consequent on the divine overtures of love? This is the question we are pursuing. We may begin by noting the defenses against historicism that an embrace of traditional Catholic christology offers.

Historicism has the tendency to sweep all of humanity's saviors under the same rug. Impressed by the diversity that human experience manifests over time, the historicist comes to doubt that anything stands out as exceptional—truly unique or of a singular order. Because there have been many people who have been acclaimed as saviors (great teachers, great saints, great exemplars of the way to healing and wisdom), and because each has been uniquely dependent on the time and culture in which he or she arose, the historicist tends to consider "salvation" a product of history. In such a view, salvation is shaped completely by the needs that a given community feel and the genius of the person they anoint savior. The savior solves their problems, pours oil on their wounds, and so heals the damage done to their sense of meaning and hope. For Indian culture, the Buddha was a great savior. For Chinese culture, Confucius and Lao Tzu stand out. Muhammad was the genius who responded to the needs of traditional Arab culture, so one can call the Qur'an that Muhammad mediated, if not Muhammad himself, the great source of salvation in Islam. Moses was the closest thing to a savior that biblical Israel knew, inasmuch as the torah mediated by Moses became the great source of healing, renewal, encouragement, and existential meaning that launched Judaism and sustained it.

The historicist understandably approaches Jesus of Nazareth in the same way that he or she approaches these other soteriological figures. Just as Muhammad adapted ideas from Judaism and Christianity to meet the needs of his Arab compatriots, so Jesus adapted ideas from the Judaism of his time to meet the needs of those hungry for something more radically fulfilling. Jesus depended on the tradition that had nourished him, even as he tried to reform that tradition. His genius is manifest in the depth that he achieved, which depth allowed his followers to transform his original address to his fellow Jews into something applicable to Gentiles as well.

We may leave it to Buddhists, Confucians, Taoists, Muslims, and Jews to express their own acceptance or rejection of the historicist outlook as it tends to interpret their traditions. Our concern is the distortions that historicism introduces into Christian convictions about Jesus. We are not denying the right of comparative religionists, working without explicit allegiance to any particular faith commitment, to treat the great figures of the world religions as they see best. We are not denying their right to treat Jesus on a par with other soteriological figures. But we are saying that historicism, or any other position that conflicts with the beliefs that have anchored the centuries of orthodox Christian worship and social service, is unacceptable on Christian theological grounds. We are saying that those who want to find the salvation promised by the Christian gospel cannot replace the traditional confessions of the full divinity and full humanity of Christ with an historicist egalitarianism.

The defenses against the reduction of Christ (from unique Son of God to merely another soteriological figure) that historicism attempts are several. First, there is the defense from spiritual experience. If one finds that worship of Christ, confession that he has the words of eternal life, love of his iconic revelation of God, and joy that in him salvation has occurred once and for all fill one's heart as the historicist perspective on Christ does not, one has good existential grounds for making traditional Christian faith, rather than the horizon of historicism (secular, critical historical interpretation), the ground of one's own life. Spiritually, the question really is which outlook brings peace, joy, and the other signs of the Holy Spirit. One is engaged in "discerning the spirits," finding which way opens one's soul, orders one's being, in face of the divine mystery, and which way does not.

But is there not a question of truth, of objective historical information, to which we must pay great heed? There is a question of truth, but we do not have to pay it great heed. The question of truth is whether there are any data about Jesus that support the claim that he was unique among the soteriological figures of world history. The answer is yes, as we have consistently tried to show by treating what Jesus taught and accomplished. This answer is not unqualified. On the basis of a purely historical analysis of Jesus (if there is such a thing), one has a hard time categorizing his miracles, his forgiveness of sin, and, above all, his resurrection. Other soteriological figures have generated claims analogous to the claims that Christians have derived from the miracles, teachings, sufferings, resurrection, and other salient features of the Jesus remembered and interpreted by the New Testament. So there is no unassailable argument from "history" (taken as an effort to comprehend Jesus apart from Christian faith) that makes it obvious that Jesus is completely unique. But there are sufficient data, sufficiently provocative claims purporting to derive from historical experience of Jesus, to ward off the counter-proposition that there was nothing unique about Jesus —were no grounds for thinking him the definitive savior or only-begotten Son of God full of grace and truth.

This means, second, that one is free to let holistic considerations determine one's commitment or noncommitment to Christ. It means, as well, that one is free to accept the traditional interpretation of the Christian community, which we have called a high or iconic christology. The holistic considerations include what praying to Jesus, filling one's spirit with the interpretation of Jesus acted out in the Christian liturgy, filling one's mind with the view of reality that faith in Jesus as the God-man has generated in Catholic Christianity, letting the teaching of Jesus shape one's sense of social responsibility, and the like do to one's personality, one's self. They also include what one finds among groups of serious Christian believers: the community or noncommunity they develop, the honesty and love they show or fail to show. Do the Christian saints strike one as appealing (in their ardor, their energy, their focus on what they considered the one thing necessary), despite their eccentricities or the inadequacies of the worldview their culture furnished them? Does Jesus himself, as one finds him in the pages of the New Testament, seem to have the words of eternal life, to be the master to whom one would love to be apprenticed, to be so great a lover of God and people like oneself that his willingness to undergo crucifixion, and the Father's raising him from death, somehow make sense?

One is free to consult the findings of investigations such as these, because no objective, supposedly scholarly assessment of Jesus can render them secondary, let alone illegitimate. One has to choose one's savior in faith, asking again and again what way of life, what modeling of divinity, one finds most beautiful, most realistic, most fitting. Similarly, one is free to accept the traditional Christian interpretations of Jesus if they sharpen one's sense of who Jesus actually was and is, increasing his attractiveness. Nothing in the historians' findings about Jesus, or even about the development of Jesus' church, vetoes the possibility that a Johannine, or a Pauline, or even a synoptic interpretation of Christ as the definitive revelation and savior given by God is the best—most useful, most compelling, most vivifying—commitment on which to build a human existence. One may in good conscience choose the Catholic Christian vision of creation, humanity, and divinity as the vision one wants to pursue, because nothing in history can prove it is false and nothing in history is obviously superior to it—least of all the vision one gets when one raises historicism to the status of a worldview (a religion) and chooses to believe there is no infinite divinity or absolute salvation available to human beings.

On Making Unlimited Commitments

What is it that allows the Christian, in good conscience, to single out one event in history and make that the be-all and end-all of his or her existential stance? How can it be that a human being, Jesus, can rightly elicit true worship: dedication due only to God? In part the answer is mysterious, because the question concerns how human beings grapple with the divine mystery—the holy plenum they can never understand and must always deal with in faith. But in part the answer is ostensible, can point to experiences that keep Christian commitment from being irrational. Let us try to elaborate such experiences.

The experiences are similar to falling in love. People are wise in their loves if they consult what prudence, reasonable investigation, reports but are willing to go beyond it, taking a risk that the goodness, the beauty, they perceive holistically is not deceptive. So, it is a "good" falling in love if the beloved is intelligent, virtuous, healthy in spirit and body, as well as mysteriously attractive. The parallel with a "good" commitment to Christ in faith is that the final "reason" for the commitment transcends anything prudential, even though it is in part justified because the needs of prudential reason have been met. In other words, Jesus is not crazy, not depraved, not proposing a program that will aggrandize himself and deplete the believer. But the full "reason" for commiting oneself to him is the self-validating experience of what happens when one lets oneself love him, his Father, and their Spirit. What happens is that one finds both contentment and challenge, both rest and incitement to continue on. What happens is that one finds a flesh and blood localizing of the desires one had (partly unawares) to embrace beauty, idealism, healing, poetry, utter honesty, holiness, prayer, and the so many other facets of human fulfillment that Jesus manifests. Finally, what happens is that Jesus turns the tables, becoming not simply the fulfillment of one's needs and hopes but their elevation, their sublation, to a new level. In the company of Jesus, "needs" and "hopes" are transformed. One sees how much more needy one actually was than one ever appreciated. One sees the depths of sin and meaninglessness. And one sees hope unbounded, stretching out to embrace infinity, eternity, and all the other aspects of the unconditioned love of God.

Thus, one can make unlimited commitments when space and time present an object, a person, who escapes from the limits of space and time. One can make unlimited commitments when the Word of God has taken flesh. The signs that something fleshly is conveying the Word of God are themselves incarnational. On the one hand, Jesus (or scripture, or the church, or the sacraments) is utterly concrete and specific, fully human and historical. On the other hand, Jesus mediates divinity (holy mystery without bounds) so perfectly that it becomes clear, sensed, that Jesus himself is such divinity. The experience that allows one to make unlimited commitments in good conscience therefore has the same structure as the incarnation with which it is aligned. The God who cannot be grasped, but who does give divinity into the keeping of creatures, meets one in Christ and carries one away in love. This being carried away, having one's mind and heart take wing, is always tied sufficiently to specific times and places to keep one's feet on the ground. It is not acosmic or gnostic, not a spiritual "trip" or self-indulgent ecstasy. If the divine spirituality present in Jesus meets and perfects the human being's deepest needs for transcendence, the full humanity of Jesus meets and perfects the human being's needs for rootage, embodiment, fidelity to the earth.

The history of christology is filled with errors on both sides of this razor's edge where divinity and humanity unite hypostatically. Some have so stressed the divinity of Christ that they have lost the humanity necessary to anchor Christ and faith in the real world. Others have so stressed the humanity of Christ that they have lost his divinity, what makes him unique and opens the salvation that only the One God could give. The commitment necessary to find the salvation that humanity needs has to embrace both the nearness of Jesus and what we might call his farness, the beyond of his strict divinity. The posture of spirit necessary to enter into the treasury of Christ's mysteries is kneeling with open arms and rapt spirit. By kneeling, one stays in touch with the earth and eschews any prideful self-exaltation. By opening one's arms one signifies both one's desire to be filled with God's Spirit and the outreach of one's own spirit in prayer. By letting one's spirit be rapt into the otherworldly mysteries of God, one honors the transcendence of God, who is never captured by the world, who is always greater.

To be sure, there are many valid postures for prayer, and we are not trying to canonize kneeling with open arms. We are simply searching for figures that suggest the twofold allegiance of Catholic spirituality, to both matter and spirit, both earth and heaven. We could use sacramental imagery to the same end. The water poured at baptism is really water: wet, liquid, cleansing. Yet it conveys spiritual washing and the influx of grace. The wine drunk at the Lord's supper is really wine: fermented, full of taste, relaxing. Yet it slakes the spirit and represents Christ's blood, shed for the forgiveness of sins. One uses such signs to make commitments, convey acts of trust and love, that go beyond anything merited by the material side of the sign. How can water bestow forgiveness of sins? How can wine bestow divine life? Only by becoming an occasion and means for the human being to receive the impress or inrush of divinity and respond with an outflow of grateful love. Only by actualizing the principles of the iconography elaborated in a high christology. On the principles of a low christology, one has only signs. Sacraments, real symbols actualizing what they signify, depend on the divine Word's identification with Jesus.

What are the benefits, and what the dangers, of making an unlimited commitment to Christ? The benefits include finding the still point of the turning world, finding that the center does indeed hold, finding that time and space are not chaotic but have a wonderfully simple, elegant, yet still disturbing order. The simplicity and elegance express the gracefulness of grace—the beauty and gentility of God's having entered time to give time a transcendent meaning. The disturbance springs from the cruciform pattern that God's order has assumed. One way of characterizing Christian spirituality is as an ongoing effort to understand how the cross could be God's chosen way of making history successful, beautiful, the comedy trumpeted in the resurrection.

The dangers of making an unlimited commitment to Christ include not appreciating what one is in for, not realizing that God is bound to take one far beyond what one initially bargained for. Then, unless one is willing to keep growing, keep walking Christ's way in pain, one can lose heart and perhaps end up in a worse state than one was in at the beginning. Superficial Christian faith is a contradiction in terms, no matter how frequently one sees it attempted on television. The difference between simplicity, which can be deep, and superficiality, which is bound to be shallow, is enormous. So Jesus tells his followers to calculate before they start to build their towers. He knows that when the iconography of the incarnation, the full art of the kingdom, takes hold, one is bound to find the world dangerous as well as wonderful, a place one has to quit as well as a place newly recognized as one's birthright.

One Christ in Ten Thousand Faces

The effort to understand how Christ can be present outside the borders of institutional Christianity is helped by the same incarnational balance that anchors unlimited commitments in the world of space and time. In keeping with the generous view of grace that a high christology associates with the Johannine theology, where the Word's taking flesh is the essence of salvation, one can think that wherever people are progressing toward full humanization, Christ is in their midst and hearts. Full humanization implies and requires the balanced love of both matter and spirit, both earth and heaven, that the incarnation reveals to be God's own love. Because human beings have to struggle for their humanity, not having it given to them the way plants and animals are given their natures, the dialectic of sin and grace that Christians associate with the triumph of Jesus may be seen at work in all people's lives.

The fact that human beings have to become what they are makes humanistic studies intriguing. It is possible for men and women to fail to become human as their natures postulate. Most legal codes grant young human beings considerable time in which to acquire sufficient maturity of judgment to be held fully accountable for their actions. Philosophers such as Aristotle have offered the opinion that fifty years are required before one is competent to make ethical judgments, because without fifty years' worth of experience one is unlikely to know how general principles ought to be applied to specific cases. The great investment that the human species has in education flows from this feature of the human condition. The less a given culture values education, the less it appreciates the struggles necessary to acquire wisdom and virtue. Some images of education liken it to an extension of procreation, and the idea has considerable merit. Just as there is an epigenesis in the womb, so there is a schedule for the knowledge and virtue that a child, an adolescent, a young adult has to meet if a morally healthy individual is to emerge. Christian instinct has long associated this schedule with the pedagogy of the Holy Spirit. Given to the child at baptism, given again in the strengthening sacrament of confirmation, the Holy Spirit works in the developing conscience to bring about a connaturality between the values of Christ and the values of the person being educated. If the person prays, reflects, worships communally, learns the tradition, studies the saints, and so forth, gradually he or she acquires "the mind of Christ" that Paul desired.

For the Greek fathers of the church, this pedagogy, along with a deep appreciation of the presence of the Logos throughout creation, suggested that being human and being Christian coincided. Without denying that many people failed to achieve their humanity, the Greek fathers were hopeful that the kinship between the wisdom of Christ and the wisdom of the best pagans would gradually become clear. In their understanding of divinization (*theosis*), the Greek fathers considered the goal of human existence to be a Christian version of the Platonic ideal: to become as much like God as possible. Thus, they tended to

think that any virtue, beauty, cooperation, or other human achievement could be correlated with Christ, could even be attributed to
Christ. Just as Christ was the fulfillment of the wisdom sketched by the
Old Testament, so he was the fulfillment of the wisdom glimpsed by
the best Gentiles. To be Christian was to find in explicit terms and
through divinization the humanization all human beings were seeking
implicitly.

For today's expanded sense of the stage on which the drama of
humanization is being acted out, these patristic notions are interesting
stimuli. Suppose that everywhere people are striving for a balanced love
that will honor both time and eternity. Suppose that those who err by
over-honoring the flesh, and those who err by over-valuing the spirit,
can both be corrected by the paradigmatic humanity of the iconic
Christ. It follows that christology offers the criteria for analyzing the
humanity that a given culture, or a given individual, is or is not achieving. If so, one can say, always and everywhere, that the balance exemplified by Christ is the ideal.

Christ loved his people, his land, the lilies of the field. Nothing in
his teaching was ascetical in the sense of despising the flesh or doubting
the goodness of creation. He put himself out for his brothers and sisters,
making their healing, their instruction, their liberation a daily concern.
It is easy to consider Jesus a strong advocate of social justice, following
in the tradition of the Israelite prophets. It is easy to consider him a
realist, convinced that God does not take people away from their flesh
and blood responsibilities, from the demands of citizenship, from the
need to make a robust culture that would incline them to pursue what is
genuinely good.

Equally clearly, however, Jesus was passionately involved with a
God who transcended space and time. Equally clearly, Jesus considered
the spirit more significant than the flesh, the heart more important
than the external deed, fidelity to conscience more significant than
preserving one's material goods. Jesus died because he kept faith with
the message his Father had given him. Jesus prayed because nothing
this-worldly could satisfy his deepest hunger. The signs that Jesus
worked suggested that one could not capture his identity in this-worldly
terms. The death that Jesus died was unearthly, as the symbolism with
which the synoptic gospels surround it indicates. And, above all, the
resurrection of Christ revealed the heavenly dimension of his signifi-

cance. He lived his fullest life in the company of his Father, whose presence was the gist of heaven and beatitude.

Wherever people are fighting the good fight to gain the balance that their humanity requires and Jesus most fully revealed, the grace of God flowing from the victory of Jesus that secured this balance is in play. That is the Christian understanding of the causality of humanization, the Christian understanding of how human goodness comes about. People open themselves to what they consider the better voices of conscience. They are willing to sacrifice lesser goods for greater goods. They are willing to love, beyond what they can prove will be to their personal advantage. In doing these quintessentially human things, they fill out the model sketched by Christ. Indeed, for Christian faith, in doing these quintessentially human things they depend on the helper whom Jesus sent into the midst of his disciples. The Holy Spirit functioning for the followers of Jesus much as Jesus functioned for the disciples while he was with them in the flesh may be imagined to be at work wherever people are battling sin and trying to say yes to grace. The Spirit is not constrained to institutional channels, any more than the risen Christ is. Both are free of the limitations of flesh and history. Both can be more intimate to human beings than those human beings are to themselves.

So in ten thousand faces, minds, hearts, spirits, loves, the great work of Christ continues. On the model of what Jesus of Nazareth taught, exemplified, and became in his resurrection, human beings everywhere are engaged with the solicitations of God. God is calling all people to follow the light rather than the darkness, to love rather than hold back, to believe that their lives can be meaningful beyond measure, perhaps especially when they encounter suffering. Jesus was so much the everyman, the complete human being, that what he manifested can be considered the goal and illumination of all human lives. By virtue of his union with God, Jesus was so consummately human that he broke the old molds and became the new one. For people who confess him to be savior and Lord, what it means to grow in wisdom and grace before God and other human beings takes its definition from Jesus. In all achievements of humanity the gracefulness of Christ is present, while in all the sufferings, the inner divisions, of sin the ugliness of rejecting the love of God revealed in Christ is plain. Everywhere, then, one can apply the paradigms of revelation and salvation set by the iconic Christ. Everywhere the yes he said to God, and the no he said to mammon and Satan, are the words of everlasting life.

Christ and the Cloud of Unknowing

If one studies the religious lives of many non-Christians, and also many Christians, it appears that the primary way in which God appears and is experienced is negative. What impresses a great many people mesmerized by the divine mystery is that one can never get it in focus. It remains. It is always there, furnishing the horizon for all thinking and the ground for all being. Yet one can never get one's words, one's mind, around the divine mystery. One can never "comprehend" it. The light has shone in the darkness, and the darkness has never comprehended it. This Johannine precept, which confesses the primordial character of God's truth, and the victory of that truth (Jesus) over all the sinful resistance the world has mustered, takes on ironic overtones when one moves it into mystical realms. The light has shone in the darkness, but the darkness (of human sin, folly, and finitude) has never been able to grasp it. Indeed, to human beings the light of God has itself seemed a great darkness. For the human mind, made to know intelligibilities housed in or communicated by matter, the pure spirituality of God is incomprehensible. The simplicity of God defeats the human intellect, which is used to analyzing complex wholes into component parts. Equally, the goodness of God defeats the human moral judgment. Used to dealing with beings impelled by self-interest, the human moral judgment does not know what to make of a divinity that is completely self-giving. If one can believe the New Testament, the Pharisees who encountered Jesus had precisely this problem. Jesus was frightening, dangerous, because one could not grasp his "angle." What was it that he was after, what power or self-aggrandizement did he seek? The Pharisees couldn't comprehend a man who wanted only to publish the kingdom of God. They didn't know what to make of a man who feared no human authority, who communed with God directly and was so intimate with God as to call him "Father."

Thus there is a great "unknowing" that Christian discipleship can entail, and many of the best writers on prayer have likened it to having a cloud come over one's mind. The presence of God is too simple, too thick, too primordially real for the intellect to handle. No words can express what God means, and no words can carry the love that the human heart wants to give back to God in response. So the person praying to God frequently is reduced to simply abiding in the cloud of God's presence, simply letting his or her heart beat in desire for God, gratitude toward God, and hope someday to see God face to face. It is a peculiar experience. As soon as one starts to think, imagine, speak, or develop any expression of love, the cloud wraps around one's mind and brings it to a halt. The lesson seems to be that only being to being communion with God, only simple presence to presence, is whole or basic enough to be satisfying. The lesson seems to be that God is pure spirit and must be worshiped in spirit and truth.

Needless to say, this experience, elaborated in slightly different terminology by John of the Cross, who made famous the notion of a "dark night" of the soul, does not conflict with the sacramental life of the church, with scripture, with worship of the iconic Christ, or with any of the other consequences of the incarnational presence of God by which Christianity stands. The great warrant for thinking that the darkness, the silence, the intangibility of God can be the presence of the divine primordiality is the preaching and being of Jesus Christ. The great teaching about the presence in believers' hearts of the incomprehensible Father, Son, and Spirit is the "high priestly prayer" of Jesus in the second half of the gospel of John. Strangely, yet characteristically, the gospel that is the most incarnational is also the most mystical. In the second half of the gospel of John Jesus himself is lost in contemplative dialogue with his Father, and although he speaks eloquently, one senses that even this incomparable speech fails to render the immediacy and richness of the relationship he is experiencing. The words seem to run behind the reality, the love. The bond between Father and Son is so basic and fulfilling that the words merely give us a clue, merely point us in the right direction.

It is the entire life of Jesus, including his death and resurrection, that suggests the complete reality that the wholly spiritual God had for him. The Father was the basis of Jesus' self-understanding. Apart from his relationship with the Father, whose will was his meat and drink, Jesus would not have known who he was. Indeed, without his relationship to the Father Jesus would not have been himself. His relationship to the Father defined his being, gave him his identity. What we see in Jesus' complete dedication to his Father's will is the human redundance or overflow of the relation that defines the eternal Word. The eternal

Word is completely defined by his derivation from the Father. He simply is the self-expression of the Father. The only thing that distinguishes him from the Father is that the Father is the original possessor of divinity and he is the originated possessor. Outside of time, with no temporal priority or subsequence, the Father has a primacy in possession of the divine fullness and the Son a dependence. But the two are oriented to one another exhaustively, inseparably. Their relationship makes each who he is. Their relationship also explains the Holy Spirit, who flows, proceeds, forth from it as their mutual love. If the Son is the self-knowledge of the Father, the Spirit is the self-love of Father and Son. Needless to say, there is nothing selfish, in our earthly sense, in the divine love. It is completely self-giving. The self-sacrifice of Jesus therefore is another exact expression in human terms of his trinitarian origins. What Jesus does in laying down his human life fits the altereity, the other-orientedness, of all three of the divine persons.

For the humble human person lost in the darkness of the divine immensity at prayer, these trinitarian convictions of Christian faith should be most consoling. The mystery, the darkness, is present only for love and self-giving. God can only be toward creatures what divinity is in itself: truth and goodness, knowing and loving. So the person being taken into the cloud should account the experience something both positive and purifying. It is positive because God is giving the person a taste of the divine purity, immediacy, simplicity. Spirit to spirit, heart to heart, God is speaking without words and figures, is communicating more directly than any symbols can. The experience is purifying because it is weaning the person away from symbols, ideas, even feelings. There is a limit to such weaning, because to be human is to depend on flesh, feelings, ideas, and symbols. Yet in the cloud of unknowing God is teaching the person to relativize all such symbols. As solid Catholic teaching has long insisted, we can never say what God is. Indeed, even when we speak fully faithfully and truly about God, God is more unlike than like what we say, because of the chasm between creator and creature.

So in the cloud of unknowing Christ becomes all the more precious. Clinging to his iconographic revelation of the goodness of God, the person whose mind is overshadowed can try simply to love. It could not be that Christ would deceive his followers about the goodness of God. It could not be that what seems to the devout person merely darkness is not paradoxically the too-bright light of God. And even when the darkness is oppressive, because we are out of sorts and our sinfulness is depressing, Jesus gives us the reason to believe and hope that we are not in a void but a great fullness. If Jesus could endure the agony in the garden and the abandonment of the cross, we should be able to endure the revelation of our nothingness apart from God. Abiding in the cloud, not fleeing such revelation, begging the support of the Holy Spirit, we may discover that the Spirit of Christ is taking over our prayer, with sighs too deep for words, and that the movement of our spirits is taking us into the eternal communication of divinity itself, where Father, Son, and Spirit are always present to one another immediately, "heart to heart," in utterly mutual knowing and loving. The speech of the Johannine Jesus and the prayer of the synoptic Jesus sanction our believing all of this.

Christ and Compassion

Human beings suffer in many ways, and for nearly all of them the iconic Christ is a great comfort and remedy. Although Jesus himself did not sin, he suffered the effects of original sin and the sins of his contemporaries, so he knew all too well how evil rebellion against God is. From this experience, which his Father made the vehicle for overcoming sin and death, Jesus may be believed to have gained the utmost compassion for the sufferings of his fellow human beings. In its devotion to the Sacred Heart of Jesus, modern Roman Catholic spirituality developed a powerful symbolism for the compassion of Christ. As early as the epistle to the Hebrews, however, the Christian community had available a language for imagining the intercessions of a high priest who identified with all of its needs. In the book of Revelation, more wonderful imagery lay ready to hand. As the Lamb who was slain for the redemption of human beings, Jesus stood in the court of heaven as a permanent memorial to the divine compassion.

The gospels have been described as the story of the passion of Christ amplified by a few preliminary descriptions of Jesus' work. That description is an exaggeration, but there is no doubt that all of the evangelists found the deepest revelation of the divine nature and will in the sufferings of Christ, as those sufferings were clarified by Christ's resurrection. It was the sufferings of Christ, his defeat in worldly terms, that put his teaching and ministry into bold relief. It was the triumph that came out of those sufferings that convinced the early Christians of the divine wisdom. What was only folly to human beings had been God's chosen instrument of salvation. What was a stumbling block to Jews and to Gentiles foolishness was the power and wisdom of God. In the light of the sufferings and triumph of Christ, the sin of Adam—the whole disordered state of humankind—could seem like a happy fault, a *felix culpa*. The grace of God so abounded over the sin of human beings that God seemed justified, magnified, by the wondrous effects of Christ's cross.

Buddhists love the compassion of the Buddha, and rightly so. Gautama spent his ministerial career, traditionally accounted about forty years, teaching a way to overcome suffering. Nothing was more important to him than helping human beings escape from the ravages of time, karma, death, desire, and the other great sources of pain. In Christian perspective, Gautama can be considered a great mercy of God, a savior who has shown hundreds of millions of Asians a way to cope with their trials. He can also be considered less personally identified with suffering than Jesus because his life was much longer and more serene. Gautama detached himself from human affairs, so that he stood apart from success and failure. Certainly his life's work stands as a great monument to his benevolence toward other human beings, but he was not crucified for his convictions. He did not confront or trouble the evildoers of his day the way that Jesus confronted his contemporaries, and he did not die in shame, like a criminal, as Jesus did. The bodhisattva vow that seized the imagination of Mahayana Buddhists, according to whom a Buddha-to-be would determine to postpone entry into nirvana and continue to labor for the salvation of all living things, is a wonderful tribute to the comprehensiveness that many Buddhists have intuited that compassion ought to develop, and one can say that it would be painful to remain in *samsara*, the realm of karmic bondage, rather than enter the bliss of nirvana. The epistle to the Philippians expresses a similar appreciation when it speaks of the emptying that Jesus was willing to experience in order to share our human condition and end up on the cross. Still, there is no figure in the history of religions comparable to Christ on the cross. Nowhere else has a paramount religious leader been so sundered and humiliated because of his message and love.

For many of the Christian saints, the price that Jesus was willing to pay was a very personal benefaction. It was for them, in all their particularity, that Jesus had died. No one had greater love for them, because no one else had laid down life for them as Jesus had. So they wept when they contemplated the cross of Christ, and their tears came from joy as much as sorrow. They were sorry that their beloved Lord had had to suffer so grievously, and doubly sorry that their own sins had helped bang in the nails. But they were also overjoyed that God should have been so good, both in being willing to suffer to redeem their sins and in turning the passion of Christ into a great triumph. Transfixed by the crucified Christ, such saints knew they had to go and do likewise. They had to lay down their lives for their brothers and sisters because of what Christ had done for them. The Johannine Jesus, resurrected and giving Peter his marching orders, spoke of feeding the flock who would gather around the gospel. The saints who spent themselves preaching, teaching, tending the sick, and missionizing those who had yet to hear the good news worked in this tradition. Whenever their spirits flagged, they could look to their crucified Lord as a source of renewed determination to feed Jesus' flock.

As much as the example of the crucified Lord tends to shame the honest observer, it should also be a great comfort. There is no depth of pain or sense of abandonment that Christ did not plumb and so does not know. There is no fear or loss or even shame that he cannot imagine. The compassion, the solidarity in suffering, symbolized by the cross is a milestone in the history of religions. If other traditions have tried to imagine how divinity is present in such negativities as death and destruction, Christianity has been signal for personalizing the entrance of God into the pain and muck of human sin. Jesus "became" sin, knew sin to its marrow, because that was what loving human beings enough to change their essential condition required. One can say, then, that the compassion Jesus showed the reputed sinners of his day, the whores and tax collectors, the sick and demented whom many orthodox said must have merited their punishment, took a universal form in the crucifixion. There divinity itself put aside the repugnance sin has to cause it and looked to the sinner's need rather than his or her just deserts. If God were to consider only justice, few would pass muster. If God depended on appreciation, salvation would still be stuck in first gear. No, God is in labor for the world's salvation because of God's own goodness and compassion. Salvation is gratuitous in the sense that all of the initiative and efficacy comes from God. The Protestant reformers who thought this truth was being compromised by the sacramental system developed in the middle ages were forced to raise an outcry. Only God is good enough to rescue human beings from their sin. Only the goodness of God published on the cross shows the depth of human need and the unexpectable willingness of God to meet it.

Once again, appreciations such as these are the major reason that those well versed in Christian tradition are bound to reject many apparently precipitous moves to make Jesus just another of the world's soteriological figures. Such Christians are bound to think that the people attempting such moves have never appropriated the depth or breadth or height of the Christian gospel. It is true that Buddhist or Muslim or other religionists who have deeply penetrated their tradition may feel that their great hero is similarly unique. However, that doesn't excuse Christians from keeping faith with the incomparable treasures their tradition has found in the compassion of Jesus. Neither does it forbid or make impossible honest dialogue among adherents of different traditions about their different understandings of the divine compassion, salvation, revelation, or anything else central to the human condition they share. In fact, it probably facilitates such dialogue by freeing the adherents of the different traditions to speak fully honestly about where their own hearts lodge.

How To Evaluate Leaps in Being

Looking at history from the heart of their commitment to Christ, Christians know implicitly the criterion they should apply to instances of revelation, salvation, and divinization occurring outside of explicit Christianity. Eric Voegelin has developed a sophisticated philosophy of history in terms of what he calls "leaps in being."[1] For Voegelin, the key moments that should structure our understanding and periodization of history are the times when humanity's constitution by the luring of God has become most clear. Israelite revelation and Greek philosophy (love of wisdom) stand out in Voegelin's tally book. In Israelite revelation, the human spirit learned that it only comes to right order by making love of the world-transcending God its great passion. In Greek philosophy, the human mind learned that it only comes to right order by making love of the Beyond its great passion. Both of these experiences were leaps in being in the sense that they took human beings to a new level of existence. They were equivalent in that both contained the realization that the natural world is not the measure of reality and that the divinity that transcends the natural world moves in the depths of the human personality to free it from idolatry and sensuality, so that it will know that God alone is its rightful treasure. Thus the Hebrew Bible mounted a fierce campaign against idolatry and both Plato and Aristotle conceived of the human vocation as to become as much like divinity as possible.

One can find parallels to the effects of Israelite revelation in Christianity and Islam. Similarly, one can find parallels to the effects of Greek philosophy in Judaism, Christianity, Islam, Hinduism, and Buddhism. Christianity and Islam both accepted the Jewish critique of idolatry, though Christian incarnationalism qualified it. Greek love of wisdom became the infrastructure of Christian speculation, Muslim speculation, and much Jewish speculation. The Indo-European mentality that Hinduism and Buddhism originally shared with Greek philosophy explains the fascination of all three bodies of speculation with the movements of the human mind toward divinity. For all three, the relationship between being and knowing came to its crucial focus in a spirituality that humanity and divinity shared somehow.

The point to using these leaps of being (and one might consider the insights of Confucius and Lao Tzu candidates for equal respect) to structure one's understanding of what human beings have learned through time about the basic constitution of their condition is that they provide a crisp criterion for determining order (realism, the outlook that has the best chance of making human beings achieve justice toward nature, divinity, other people, and their own selves). When people realize that the divine beyond is the great source of wisdom and fulfillment in human affairs, they can stand free of the oversights and idolatries that tend to warp all their significant relationships. If God is the great treasure, and one may only "gain" vivifying contact with God through worship in spirit and truth, then money, power, fame, possessions, and all the other things to which human beings tend to look for their justification, their worth, are all secondary. When they fall into place behind God, as lesser treasures, they can be precious and lead people further to praise God as wise and good. When people attempt to replace God with them, they become idols and make such people unrealistic, disordered, spiritually diseased. Wars, economic inequities, political disenfranchisements, and the various other species of injustice stem from such spiritual disease. Take the ungraspable divinity from the center of human evaluation and you have made it impossible for human beings to live well, in truth and love. That is the gist of a Voegelinian analysis of history in terms of history's great leaps in being. For Voegelin the Nazi and Stalinist atrocities were the great negative proofs of the validity of this analysis.

Christian students of history are bound to be impressed by this analysis and wonder how it correlates with the iconic Christ at the center of their faith. It correlates quite well. First, one notes that Christianity consciously combined Israelite revelation and the Greek love of wisdom into the foundations of its theology—its basic understanding of God and reality. Though the New Testament is more Jewish than Greek in its religious conception. Hellenism still remains a potent influence. The apologists who tried to defend Christianity against its detractors and explain it to people looking for salvation came into their own in the second century. At that time such thinkers as Justin Martyr and Clement of Alexandria proposed that Christ was not only the fulfillment of the Hebrew scriptures but also of the best of pagan longing. In other words, Christ was not only the messiah but also the embodiment of the wisdom that Socrates, Plato, Aristotle, and the other pagan luminaries had sought. The key to the great value of Christ was his perfect balance as the enfleshment of divinity that saved and perfected humankind. He was both the authorized revealer of the beyond (the Father) luring all people's hearts and minds, and the exemplar of what a humanity ordered by passionate love of this beyond would be like. In his death and resurrection, he had solved the great problem that had afflicted human beings like a curse from their beginnings. By making divine wisdom fully human, a thing of parables, healings, and personal relationships that people could contemplate inexhaustibly, Jesus had provided precisely what humanity, made of flesh and spirit, needed. The worship he had inspired appealed to all the senses, teaching even the unlettered about the love and service of God. The community he had inspired sought a fellowship of love and service that would make belonging to Christ the gateway to a new society, a new culture, and a new politics. Nothing human was foreign to Christ, because Christ had been fully human. Yet nothing divine was now foreign to humanity, because in Christ the Logos had taken humanity into the divine embrace, joining with it hypostatically, personal substance to personal substance.

As the heirs of this tradition, which of course was greatly enriched as well as occasionally sidetracked through the succeeding centuries, today's Catholic Christians can be confident that they have a well-tested criterion for evaluating claims about revelation, progress, wisdom, salvation, and the like. If a claim squares with the leap in being, the delineation of the divine and human natures in their correlation, accomplished in Christ, it deserves careful attention. If it makes God the great treasure and measure, while loving human flesh as the sacramental expression of God, it offers wisdom and healing. Claims that would close history, natural or human, to divinity, arguing that God is an error or an irrelevance, should be rejected out of hand (though analyzing why intelligent people could put forward such claims can be highly instructive). Claims that Christ is not the great icon of God and the crossroads where divinity and humanity meet most revealingly should also be rejected out of hand, because they clash with what Christians have to believe is the crucial leap in being, the fullest revelation and salvation. And claims that human beings are not sacramental presences of God, places where natural history and human events alike find their greatest significance, should be rejected out of hand, because they play false to the humanism consequent on the incarnation. This does not mean a license to despise nature or pollute the ecosphere. It does mean a conviction that human flesh has best shown the love that God is, and that the love that God is is creation's reason to be.

I-Thou Relations with Jesus

We turn now to some of the implications that the position we have been advancing about the uniqueness of the iconic Christ holds for Catholic Christian spirituality. First, how may one relate to the Christ who is the personal presence of the love of God that works human beings' salvation and divinization? Is there any room within the adoration that his divine status warrants for fully personal, I-Thou relations? The answer is yes, there is much room for fully personal, I-Thou relations with the iconic Christ. Indeed, the mysteries of Christ's earthly life are available as limitless opportunities to reflect on the love God has shown human beings and let this love occupy the center of one's heart and life.

The man Jesus impressed his contemporaries as someone with whom to reckon. Those who resented his words and deeds tended to account him a dangerous enemy, but those who found light and solace in his words and deeds found themselves drawn ever more deeply into the intrigue of his person and work. Jesus was not a man who delivered himself up for easy comprehension. On first meeting, it was not at all apparent what he was up to or what his measure was. The more one tried to take the measure of him, the more one found him taking one's measure in return. He could not be subsumed under any of the categories available at his time. He was not just a prophet, or a rabbi, or a mystic, or a political reformer, or a healer, or the leader of a new religious movement. He was all of these things, but none of them summed him up. Even if one put all these categories together, and added such other categories as messiah, Jesus spilled out of one's containers and remained much more. He was an original, someone who both broke the old molds and became himself the new mold.

For those who want to know Jesus not simply as a literary or historical or even theological figure, but as a living reality, the words and deeds presented in the gospels assume the status of a personal invitation: "Come and see." Just as prospective disciples could follow Jesus, spend time with him, hear how he responded to different questions, and slowly get a feel for what his way of life implied for new problems, so latter-day followers of Jesus can frequent the pages of scripture and learn what St. Paul called "the mind of Christ." Understandably, their principal focus should be the New Testament, but they may also follow the authors of the New Testament and the church fathers in finding the Old Testament relevant to their undertaking, especially the servant songs of Isaiah 40–55. As they read relevant scriptural passages slowly, pondering and digesting them, such latter-day followers or inquirers can imitate the original disciples in asking Jesus questions about why he says or does what he does. They can also imitate the original disciples in finally quieting their tongues and minds, shutting off their imaginations, and simply gazing at Jesus in appreciation, simply trying to see him in the round and let the love that such seeing stimulates take over their hearts.

The gist of an I-Thou relationship is that one opens one's heart, one's fully existential self, and asks for entrance to the other person's heart. One is not satisfied with superficial, formal acquaintance. Workaday familiarity will not do. One wants to know who the other person really is, and one wants to be known that way in return. Even though much of what one seeks in an I-Thou relationship is a better understanding of one's own self, the main accent has to be on speaking to the other with a desire to meet the other's real self—not out of curiosity, but from a desire to know and love the other's personal truth. It follows that I-Thou relationships are difficult and rare. They cannot be prosecuted casually. In asking to know another person this profoundly, one pledges to be faithful to any revelations that follow—to honor the secrets they carry and deal gently with the vulnerabilities they manifest.

All this holds for the Christ one may meet in the mysteries recorded in the New Testament and presented in the Christian liturgy. Solemn as both scripture and liturgy can be, the human Jesus who speaks from their pages or ceremonies invites great intimacy. As Jesus himself puts it, he has not called his followers servants but friends, because he has revealed to them all the secrets of his heart. He has not kept anything back. What he could express and they could understand he has made over to them. Indeed, he has made over to them more than they could understand before his death and resurrection, as an act of trust that later they would find everything fall into place.

It is true that the Jesus one contemplates saying these things is a product of a generation or more's memory and worship. It is true that the Jesus available in the New Testament is presented from the perspective of people who knew and believed that the Father had raised him from the dead, in testimony to the victory of his way and person. But this simply reminds us that the New Testament was never meant to be a detached description of Jesus of Nazareth. Always it presupposed faith and sought to deepen faith. Always it was a book created from memories long prayed over and used in worship of God. The Christ one finds in scripture is the Christ his followers had found viable—able to center a new community, able to ground pristine good news, able to inspire worship of the Ancient of Days, the God who was and who is and who is to come.

It is worship that puts the sharpest edge on our I-Thou relations with God and Christ. It is prayer, personal or communal, that keeps religion from sliding into sapiential reflection. When one really prays, one enters upon a person to person engagement. Perhaps that is why Jesus so frequently encouraged people to bring their needs, their petitions, their pains. These were eminently real. They were the kind of thing one could not omit telling a dear friend, because they were one's self at the given time and place. Not to mention them would be to hold back on what really was going on, what actually was the truth of one's then and there self. True friends did not do that with one another. If they did hold back, they threatened their friendship, because their friendship depended on their mutual openness, their full sharing.

So, believing that the Christ heading the Christian community was permanently revealed in the gospels, the early Christians started the practice of praying to him very personally. They would relive the mysteries of his life, especially the moments of his suffering, and try to draw ever closer to the self those mysteries revealed. Solemnly, in the official liturgy, they would ask the Spirit of Christ to make them contemporaries of their Lord, so that "today" he would be born again in their midst, or "today" their own sins would be the reason he was being nailed to the cross. When Jesus spoke to Martha, or Mary, or John, or Zacchaeus up in the tree, he spoke across the centuries to the person contemplating him here and now. His words were not merely timeless truths, a *philosophia perennis*. The Spirit and the living Christ could and would ensure that they became illuminating and strengthening for the contemplator's present needs: how to pray better, how to bear up under family problems, how to prepare for death, how to think about the scandals of the church's sinfulness, or whatever.

Unless we appreciate this I-Thou, wholly personal approach to Jesus that made him a contemporary of the person seeking him out in the scriptures or at the liturgy, we will not understand why Jesus could never become just another soteriological figure. The Jesus of living Christian faith has not been an historical figure so much as a present reality. He had really lived in the past, yes, and it was useful to know the conditions of his life, but more important was his residence in people's hearts, in the tabernacle on the altar, or in pages of scripture that could change their existential import day by day and become words of everlasting life. Certainly, one can find parallels in other religious traditions, but for Christians they remain beside the point. Such parallels have to be assimilated to the experiences that give Jesus his fullest resonance and most make Christians Christians, rather than Christian experiences being assimilated to the parallels. Otherwise, one does not have the focus of faith necessary for either Christian spirituality or Christian theology. Otherwise, the cart is before the horse. Whether one tries Zen meditation, or considers Hindu notions of the avatar, or ponders the Jewish understanding of torah, or lets one's spirit go out to the Allah who is the splendid Lord of the Worlds, one's exercise is Christian in the measure that it submits everything that one gains to the judgment of Christ. Naturally, from such exercises one can deepen one's appreciation of how beautiful the judgment of Christ, the presence of the Logos revealed in Christ, actually is. But in the final analysis one cannot be schizophrenic or ambivalent about where the center of a Christian faith lies. In the final analysis, it either lies with Christ, in the trinitarian relations, or it is not Christian (with the consequence that what it means in the order of salvation is unclear).[2]

Jesus the Male

In one's contemplations of Jesus, and the I-Thou relationship one hopes to establish, the fact that Jesus was a Jewish male of the first century has to be taken into account. Because Christian faith considers Jesus to have been fully human, it implies that Jesus had a human "personality." He was himself, unique and peculiar, the product of his family background, time, place, and particular graces from God. The portrait of him that one finds in the New Testament assumes all this. It never tries to make Jesus universal in the sense of having no sharp angles, no distinguishing turns of phrase, likes and dislikes. We have called Jesus an "everyman," and we have argued that his teaching and suffering have universal application, since they serve the Father's plan for the salvation of the entire progeny of Adam. But this does not mean that Jesus wasn't born of the Virgin Mary in the time of King Herod, that he did not die under Pontius Pilate, that he didn't have specific disciples named Peter, James, Andrew, and John. The Christian understanding of Jesus says that precisely in and through this specificity the Logos of God manifested itself and the world's savior appeared, full of grace and truth. Orthodox Christology is a both/and, a dual affirmation, not an either/or. Jesus was both specific and universal, both particular and everyman. This fusion, this identity in duality, is what we have meant by an iconic christology.

Granted this, let us now reflect on one aspect of Jesus' particularity, his maleness. At another time, we could reflect on the Jewishness of Jesus, or on the influence of Jesus' time and place, or on the fact that Jesus never lived into his forties. Had we more information, we could reflect on the family lineage of Jesus, his genes and psychic inheritance. In each case, we would not be attempting to reduce Jesus to one of his aspects. Anything we learned would be only a partial illumination of a whole that remained mysterious (as the whole of every human being does, but more so in the case of Jesus, whose identity rested more profoundly in the person of the Logos). For the moment, though, let us content ourselves with reflecting on the maleness of Jesus, as an example of how a Catholic spirituality may approach the mysteries of Christ.

The people who compiled the gospels were impressed by the authority that Jesus exercised. Indeed, the authority with which Jesus spoke and worked cures was one of the first clues many onlookers had to his exceptional status. He did not try to justify his positions by elaborate exegeses of the torah, the way many a rabbi of his day would have. He did not bring forward the reputation of other teachers to bolster his own words. He simply told his hearers what the kingdom of God was like and what it required of them. In so doing, he told them, of course, what God was like and what they should become. At some points, Jesus even corrected the traditional teachings: "You have heard that it was said to men of old, 'You shall not kill; and whoever kills shall be liable to judgment.' But I say to you that everyone who is angry with his brother shall be liable to judgment. . . . You have heard that it was said, 'You shall not commit adultery.' But I say to you that every one who looks at a woman lustfully has already committed adultery with her in his heart' " (Mt 5:21–22, 27–28). The entire sermon on the mount (Mt 5–7) proceeds in this authoritative tone, as Jesus explains the fundamental spirit of the kingdom of God. The authority with which he teaches is staggering, and those who heard him divided into two camps. Some were so offended that they judged him a dangerous religious revolutionary. Others loved the power of God that went out from him.

The power that went out from Jesus when he cured the sick, gave sight to the blind, cast out demons, raised the dead, and forgave sins was even more dramatic. In the gospel of Mark, that power is pitted against the power of Satan, and eventually Jesus triumphs by taking to himself the full force of the evil that Satan can muster. Jesus is the strong man able to ward off all those attempting to possess the houses, the selves, of the people the Father has given into his keeping. He has the power of a champion, a defender of God's cause.

Now, authority and power fit the stereotype of masculinity that the majority of cultures the world over have built. In Jesus' day, Jewish culture associated the authority to teach and rule with men, giving women little access to religious learning or authority. There is nothing in the makeup of women that renders them unable to study, grow wise, or receive charismatic authority from God. There is nothing that renders them incapable of developing, receiving, or exercising religious power and so mediating God's healing, forgiveness, victory over evil, and the like. But the fact that Jesus did these things in a male body and a masculine personality fitted the cultural assumptions of his day. Once again, however, we see that Jesus changed such assumptions as much as he assimilated his work to them. Once again we see that Jesus broke the old molds and fashioned new ones.

Consider, for example, the end-product of Jesus' bold, authoritative teaching in the sermon on the mount. It greatly deepens, interiorizes, and sharpens the demands of fidelity to God. External performance is not enough. People have to respond from the heart, in full love, if they are to satisfy the God who is offering them such extraordinary newness and grace. Whether or not Jesus could have found precedents for his emphases in contemporary rabbinical teachings is a secondary point. Nothing in his portrait in the New Testament suggests that he needed or desired to be derivative or part of a school. The entire emphasis is on contemplating the significance of the kingdom and intuiting its consequences. The consequences that Jesus saw and taught, in full authority, overturned many of the assumptions, including many of the assumptions about power-relations, of the men of his day. For example, it was not enough to refrain from adultery. The spirit of the kingdom meant viewing women as full human beings, rather than as objects of desire. It was not enough to keep from killing. The spirit of the kingdom meant regretting even anger, because other people were one's brothers and sisters. In proposing such an overturning of people's going expectations, Jesus was redefining what maleness, and femaleness, entailed. He was using the boldness and power associated with vigorous men to change people's understanding of what humanity, male or female, was all about. So authority and power receded into the background, losing any great significance in their own right. What was important was the vision, the divine reality, they served. On the cross, Jesus further overturned the ordinary understanding of authority, power, success, failure, maleness, full humanity, and much more. He even overturned the notions of messiah and God. Thenceforth, those who followed Jesus would be bound to have an eye for paradoxes. Thenceforth, nothing could be taken at what the world said was its face value; everything had to be submitted to the dialectic of Jesus' judgments. That is what we mean when we say that Jesus has to be the center in any truly Christian approach to any significant understanding of human affairs—religious, political, sexual, whatever. That is why we repeat so often that Jesus cannot be simply another soteriological figure: he is for Christians the one who defines what soteriology is and can be, just as he defines what it means to be a man.

Jesus and Women's Liberation

Does the maleness of Jesus disqualify him from saving females? On the face of it this would seem to be a foolish question, but some feminists have placed it in the context of a western sexism with many debts to Christianity and so have made it respectable. If placing one's faith in Jesus as the source of one's salvation, the source of God's best disclosure about the human problematic and the divine love that can solve it, were necessarily to entail sexism, such an act of faith could be immoral. Indeed, one could say that the sexism canceled out the salvation, making the claims for Jesus contradictions in terms. Sexism is oppression and sin. Salvation is healing, liberation, and grace. There cannot be any such thing as a sexist salvation or savior.

It follows, then, that faithful Christians are virtually bound to distinguish between their savior and his followers. Jesus must have included women in his soteriological work, as the New Testament in fact shows him doing (see, for example, the interaction between Jesus and the Samaritan woman in John 4). The salvation that Jesus accomplished must have torn out the roots of sexism, just as it tore out the roots of racism, economic injustice, and all the other forms of social sin and systemic oppression. To believe in Christ is to accept such a view of all the things that twist human existence out of shape. In principle, Jesus has conquered them and made possible a new, healthy humanity. In principle, the old order of Adam, marked by alienation from God, nature, self, and other people, has passed away, and a new order, of gracious familiarity with God, has come into being. That is what belief in Christ, the messiah manifested in the resurrection, entails.

But how can there be salvation, and the possibility of women confessing Jesus to be their savior and Lord, when so much sin and distortion remain? What does it mean to confess that Jesus triumphed in the resurrection, defeating death and causing the old order of Adam to pass away, when sinful poverty, racism, sexism, warfare, and all the ugly rest remain so virulent? Perhaps it means going more deeply into the neediness of all human beings than we tend to do and realizing the liberation that comes from finding oneself able and willing to give God a blank check.

As finite and sinful, human beings are mortal and bound to suffer. These are simply elementary facts about the actual human condition. We die, and all our rightful protest against this fate does not change it. We suffer from evil and injustice, some of it of our own making, and there is no archimedian lever by which we can remove ourselves from "original sin," the systemic disorder tainting all human affairs. But if neither death nor evil is the last word, we can live by hope rather than despair. If immortality and goodness (grace, love) arguably are stronger than death and evil, the future remains open. For Christians, Christ has opened the future. In the nonpareil person, preaching, healing, suffering, dying, rising, and subsequent reign of Christ, things are more than what they seem. They may seem to be rendered hopeless by death and evil, but Christ says there is much more: not only the equally interesting presence of creativity and kindness, but also the greater strength of life and love.

Such an affirmation means that salvation has occurred. Because the human spirit can find meaning in even its worst experiences (by correlating them with the cross of Christ), nothing need make us call life a cheat, a cruel joke, something we would have been better off never to have been thrown into. To be sure, to claim that human beings can find meaning even in cancer or Auschwitz or an epidemic of drugs is liable to misunderstanding. As well, it asks people to go deeper and try harder than they are wont to do. Evil itself is a surd, something radically irrational. The meaning one can find in it can only be its redemption by a greater rationality and love. One only comes upon such a greater rationality and love when one meets the transcendent God who can be infinite light and goodness. The possibility of salvation depends on something more than human entering into human affairs and reordering them.

If one can take Jesus to heart and appropriate the iconic christology that we have proposed, the possibility of writing God a blank check comes into view. Jesus wrote a blank check to his Father: not my will but thine be done. Jesus believed that in all circumstances his God would be a loving Father, and his belief was both put to the cruelest of tests (in the crucifixion) and completely verified (in the resurrection). The faith of Christians is an imitation of Christ. Christians try to do what their Lord did, praying as he did: "Our Father . . . into thy hands I commend my spirit." Such faith can overcome the world, as the victory of Christ showed. It can lead to astounding goodness and heroism, as the lives of the saints testify. When it is strong, it produces a vision of the world in which God's love is the realest thing one knows. All of this, of course, is salvation in eminent degree. All of this is liberation from the last and worst enemies: death, the defeat of the spirit in despair.

If women most need liberation from death and the defeat of the spirit in despair, women most need the salvation offered by Christ. If women can believe in Jesus the Christ, women can receive such salvation. There seems no doubt that such liberation is women's greatest need, because all of women's hopes and projects are lost if death and the defeat of the spirit in despair have no conquerer. There seems no doubt that women can believe in Jesus the Christ, because millions have done so, many of them to stunningly humanizing effect.

But maybe these are just syllogistic games, abstract little responses to crushingly concrete problems like wife-battering, rape, systematic exclusion from fair shares in power and prosperity. Maybe women no longer can believe as their foremothers did, because now they know what men and men's religion have done to them. Maybe so, but probably not. Probably all of human beings' concrete problems run into the mystery of God and God's providence, the articulation of which can seem abstract (though often it is not). Probably women of today are not so different from women of yesterday as some of them think, even when one admits that having one's consciousness of injustices raised changes one's sense of the world significantly. Women have always been somewhat aware of sexism, and women of today seeking liberation from sexism run into the same basal mysteries as women of the past did: Why should unfairness, injustice, evil keep occurring? Why should they keep occurring even in women themselves? Who or what could deliver men and women from their bondage to such evil? How in the world, or out of the world, could love triumph over death, could life resurrect beyond suffering and evil? If women are to be liberated radically, to the roots of their pain, they will have to find symbols and powers, beliefs and practices, that do far more than make them the equals of men, or the mistresses of their own fates (bodies, psyches, morality), or any of the other good things that most women's talk and praxis about liberation target. Such symbols and powers, beliefs and practices, are needed to contend with the fact that women die, that women are guilty, that women are hungry for a fulfillment, a divinity, a love that transcends space and time, history and feminist theory. Christian faith says that Jesus offers, provides, a full response to such greatest needs. Christian faith says that despite the failings of Jesus' followers, including their malignant sexism, Jesus himself remains a viable savior—indeed, the only one with the full words of life that women or men long to hear. So Christian faith is bound to consider Jesus the crux of women's liberation. In our view, this crux is much more profound than either the nihilism to which antireligious feminist theory tends or the superficial, distorting, sinful subjugation of women to which fundamentalist Christian readings of Jesus tend. In our view, the liberation of Christ is a refining fire, offering women and men alike much more than, before it, they could even realize they needed.

Christ and Other Gurus

But does a Christian commitment, making Jesus the icon of God and so the privileged interpretation of reality, rule out learning from other teachers? Do women have to turn aside from the theorists who have clarified their malaise, their marginalization, their difficulty in achieving a solid sense of self? Do other liberationists have to turn aside from Marxist theory, which many have found helpful in clarifying the influence of economics on the divisions of societies into haves and have nots? Do people interested in international affairs have to turn aside from studies that show the significance of Hinduism in India, of Buddhism in East Asia, of Islam in Africa and the Middle East? Indeed, does anyone looking for spiritual sustenance have to give up what he or she has been finding, because Jesus ought to hold a monopoly on truth and salvation?

Obviously, the answer is no. A christology confident of the status of Jesus as the incarnate Logos can be fully Catholic: appreciative of truth and helpfulness wherever they occur. It can be reverent toward the beauty that almost all cultures have produced, when they have been allowed to develop their native instincts. It can even claim all such truth, helpfulness, and beauty for Christ, not in an imperialist sense, but in a sense of responsive gratitude. Christians need not think themselves wiser, or more capable of producing beauty, or more signal in promoting justice and peace than their fellow human beings. In the name of the savior, the revealer, the friend who has most touched their own hearts, they can praise God for not leaving divinity without trace anywhere.

So there need be no polemic between followers of the iconic, truly universal Christ and followers of other teachers, and there can be rich exchanges, both intellectual and practical. The only qualification one must place is that, to be fully Christian, the final judgment passed on any teaching, work of art, work of social service, and the like has to issue from what Jesus the Christ has meant. The word "final" in this sentence is important. The judgment in question is not a matter of aesthetics or economics. It is a matter of ultimate meaning, of redemption and divinization. When it comes to what feminist theory, or Marxist theory, or Buddhist meditation, or Muslim architecture, or recent cosmology, or any other potentially absorbing teaching or influence means for people's healing into full humanity and reception of divine life, the Christian criterion has to be Jesus.

Now, there are different ways to deploy such a criterion, and we would argue for ones that are dextrous yet fully honest. The dextrous ways take Christian convictions about the universal operation of the trinitarian persons as a stimulus to think very positively about the wisdom of the Buddha or Confucius, the beauty of a Zen garden or a feminist prayer circle. Further, they do not impose Christian patterns on these phenomena but let them express themselves in their own terms. Only after such self-expressions have occurred, and it comes time to assess what they mean for redemption and divinization, do Christian categories become imperative, and even then such self-expressions should be allowed to freshen Christians' thinking about their beloved, traditional categories (derived from the iconic Christ). Indeed, often it is new questions or angles of inquiry, prompted by dissatisfaction and pain, that stimulate the renewal of Christians' appreciation of what God has done in making Jesus the abiding sacrament of eschatological love.

The fully honest ways of deploying Christ as the criterion of final meaning explain that this is the Christian's home truth, the treasure on which the Christian's heart has been set—the reason why the Christian is a Christian. Further, they are willing to confess the personal experiences on which such an allegiance depends. Without being exhibitionist, Christians ought to be willing and able to talk about their prayer, the meaning they have found in Christian symbols, the healing that scripture and the sacraments have mediated. In doing this, Christians do open themselves to the possibility of being misunderstood and mocked, but (returning to dexterity) it is possible to be confessional without "testifying" in the ways that the mass media have made offensive. It is possible to be sober, rational, and detached: this is my truth, small as it may be, and, God help me, I can do no other. It is possible to confess one's love without seeming either pietistic or judgmental. And, finally, it is even possible to be frank about the shallowness one finds in most of the alternatives that are proposed as replacements for Christian faith.

This last point perhaps merits fuller explanation. Recently an academic friend confessed, with some rueful laughter, that a colleague had told him he was the only intellectual the colleague knew who was still a practicing Catholic. The others thought they had outgrown their cradle Catholicism, and though they might feel a little nostalgia for some parts of it, on the whole they acted as though no modern adult could take it seriously. Certainly, the grounds for such a judgment have been well surveyed: the different stupidities and inhumanities one can find among Catholics; the worldliness to which all of us are liable; the perennial difficulty of praying, living out the self-sacrificing ethics of Jesus, and contending with a God ineluctably mysterious. It is all too familiar.

What happens too seldom in that sort of exchange, however, is the Catholic party's asking for the alternative to Christian faith. What is it that the Ivy League lawyer (in this case) himself lives by? What do he and his secularized colleagues say about death, evil, the need for repairing human nature, the desires of the human heart to meet, love, and be transformed by God, the transcendent? Usually the answer is a rather superficial stoicism in which there is no ultimate meaning and so each person ought to take what measures he or she can to survive and be as happy as possible. This is the answer, in fact, that dominates current American literature, in the sense of being displayed with great skill, and gaining much critical acclaim, in the works of writers such as Richard Ford, Raymond Carver, and David Leavett.[3] But compared to the enormity of the pain that humanity suffers, and the greatness of human longing, and the visions unfurled by the great religious traditions, and the sacramental luster of Christ, it seems a pathetic answer: thin, ignorant of the best products of past cultures, and afraid to let its heart open to hope and love, lest its heart be hurt again. In a word, compared to the crucified Christ, it has little positive to say that more than scratches the surface of human potential. True, taken sympathetically, as good writers such as those just mentioned allow one to take it, this stoic view can elicit a renewed appreciation of the great need to which Christ matches up. Yet along with sympathy must come regret: if only these people, whether artful or common (or even simply hedonistic) could encounter Christ afresh, so that they could admit to themselves the better life for which they are longing and be brought to realize that even this better life is nothing compared to the love and life God has already shown them.

Jesus and the Poor

The poor in spirit, who feel that a stoic self-protection is the best defense against both human disappointment and the mystery of God, make a claim upon Christ, as do the poor in body, who suffer malnutrition, medical neglect, illiteracy, job discrimination, and a dozen other assaults on their health, their dignity, and their faith. For the poor in body, Jesus offers the revolutionary good news that God has thrown the mighty down from their thrones and set the divine heart on the "little ones." For the poor in spirit, Jesus offers the great challenge to study more deeply both human pain and human hope, to see how they converge on the crucifixion and resurrection of God's Word enfleshed.

All the different kinds of poverty relate to the Christ who emptied himself. Because of his love for the Father, Jesus was willing to keep preaching the good news of the kingdom, even when it had become clear that this would cost him his life. Because of his love for those the Father had entrusted to his care, Jesus was willing to become a sacrifice for the many. There is no sorrow or pain that God does not know—that is the message of the crucifixion. There is no human hope that God does not fulfill—that is the message of the incarnation and resurrection. If people have become so accustomed to Christian symbols that those symbols no longer carry explosive significance, we need a powerful return to basics. As actually experienced, human pain and human hope are never trite. As actually experienced, the assault on the human body or spirit that brings the person low is an outrage, crying out to God for redress. The shopkeeper robbed, the woman raped, the child abused —each has a claim on the justice and mercy of God. Similarly, the poet enraptured, the artist suddenly seeing, the scientist aware of a whole new pattern—each has a claim on the beauty and intelligibility of God. But the justice and mercy of God cannot be calculated apart from the cross of Christ. The beauty and intelligibility of God cannot be calculated apart from the iconic Christ whom God has set as the hinge between divinity and humanity. What the destruction of human flesh and spirit means depends on the message of the crucified. What the elevation of human flesh and spirit means depends on the message of the resurrected one. For Christian instinct, this is both a given and the basis for a profound humanism. For humanistic instinct that is not explicitly Christian, it should be an astringent challenge: taste and see the goodness of the Lord. Take to heart the real Christ, as one finds him in the pages of the New Testament and the experience of the saints, and see whether the problems you have been agitating and the visions you have glimpsed do not return to you wonderfully transformed.[4]

People who are aware of their poverty have a claim upon God, not simply because the biblical God has promised to be their defender, but also because the very acknowledgement of poverty opens people up to the divine help. As long as human beings claim self-sufficiency, they are limited to what their own powers can produce. Only when they realize the depth of their ignorance, mortality, and sin can they reach out to God spontaneously, fully, honestly. To say this is not to overlook the fact that self-reliance is a natural stage on the way to full maturity. It is not to propose weakness, helplessness, wringing one's hands and shuffling one's feet as signs of saintliness. But it is to say that faith, and simple humanity, remain superficial until one realizes the depths of human need. It is to say that human beings undergo far more than they initiate, that our meaning is tied more to our passion than to our action. We undergo the effects of past history, of our heredity, of our home life as children, of our environment, and of the sin of the world (the radical disorder passed down generation after generation). We undergo the limitations set by our body, our education, our range of experience, our range of friends, and even the gifts and graces God has dispensed to us. Some of us are healthy and others are fragile. Some of us are bright and others are slow. A few have grown up in warm, healthy homes and many have grown up in homes with large troubles. Out of all this passion, all this undergoing, comes the obvious truth that the providence of God has more to say about what we accomplish than we do ourselves. When one adds the monumental facts that we die, that we remain ignorant of God (condemned to struggle with divine mystery) to the end, and that we have sinned personally, our neediness rises up as the most significant thing about us.

The mercy of God goes out to meet this neediness. Because of the mercy of God, as Christ has displayed it once and for all, all of human poverty becomes a claim on God's help. Directly, the mercy of God teaches us that we should show one another mercy. If God has loved us, in good part because our need has moved the divine heart, we should love one another, in good part because we realize how vulnerable any of us is. Certainly, we should also love the strength that human beings show, and we should support the active efforts to make the earth habitable that help keep chaos and darkness at bay. Certainly, we should admire the accomplishments of Christ, what his preaching and teaching and healing produced, so that we do not shrink our christology to the cross. Yet the fact remains that such accomplishments of Christ, and the good effects reaped by human industry, continue to frame the sufferings epitomized in Christ's cross. Until human efforts can defeat death and remove sin, the great need of human beings will be not for more effort (though more effort we must have) but for more openness to the divine help that makes such effort wise and enables human beings to bear up even when their best efforts fail.

We authors remember encountering some years ago a famous political activist to whom the consolations of religion were anathema. She was convinced that women could pull themselves up by their bootstraps and that anything that diverted their attention from "the struggle" was women's enemy. But what if the struggle fails, or is a long time in succeeding, or never can remove cancer, crime, bigotry, let along ugliness and death? What if there are desires, needs, hopes in the human spirit that pass beyond the horizon of the struggle, reaching out toward a heaven that is more than an egalitarian society? The famous political activist had no answer for these questions, and no patience for them. She could only turn on her considerable dramatic ability and rage at them as subversive, weak-spirited, part of the defeatism that religion had encouraged for millennia to keep the oppressed in their place.

Yet the questions remain, as near as the actual lives of the poor. What activist program can guarantee that life will become ideal, if only we can get drunk drivers, or members of the National Rifle Association, or drug pushers, or sexist bigots off the streets and the corridors of power? We need activist programs to gain what measure of practical improvement in social conditions we can, but we also need to correlate them with a vision that can make sense of their partiality. It is not a question of either/or. It is a question of both/and. If we take Christ as our model, we will be concerned with healing broken bodies and illumining dulled minds, as well as with mediating graces of forgiveness, immortality, and divinization. If we take Christ as our model, we will be concerned with fashioning a new sense of creation, of human community, of religious institutions, and the like that holds the potential for greatly lessening the occurrence of war, economic rape, violence and destruction. And we will not blush to point out that the greatest poverty of human beings shows in their manifold vulnerability. One criminal in a neighborhood, one clot in a brain, one fool in a key organization can wreak havoc. Without a Christ to stand against such havoc, the world is bound to seem chaotic. Ruled by chance, if not malevolence, human existence is bound to seem a sadistic punishment. But Christ obviously transformed such poverty, embracing it with such trust that the Father resurrected him on the other side, in the beyond where the riches of divinity prevail. Christ obviously had words of everlasting life that rearranged the significance of all human poverty, making our main task the acquiring of ears with which to hear. That is why Christ is the savior of the world, and why the poor so regularly have been the first to acclaim him.

Jesus and Creativity

If the poor represent the majority in the world, so that Christ's sufferings and responsiveness to human neediness give him a universal significance, the creative represent something that might flower in the majority, were they freed up to hope and dream. Creativity is closely tied to love. When we are in love, we find it easy to write creative scenarios in which the beloved deserves our complete trust, respect, and service. When we are in love, the lilies of the field convey the divine care, language is always on the verge of poetry, people are more to be admired than despised. Love of their work and the natural world it reveals keeps scientists in their laboratories, where they sharpen their good minds and occasionally enjoy the ecstasy of solving a significant problem and wondering, in brute, open-mouthed awe, at the intricacy and beauty of the universe. Love of other people took the great saints, east and west, to transports of insight and compassion, convincing them that one could not separate the divine, the best they could conceive, from the drama of simple human beings struggling to gain their humanity. In the grip of love, parents have found novel ways to save and help their children, artists have spent their time serving the liege-lady beauty, and ordinary believers have gone to their knees, confessed their sins, and asked their liege-Lord to help them do better. Inasmuch as we take Christ to be the sacrament, the iconic presence, of the divine love, healing and elevating, we prime ourselves to bring creativity into relationship with Jesus of Nazareth, his Father, and the Spirit who led him into the wilderness to become the great benefactor of humankind.

The effort to rethink the relationship between Jesus and other soteriological figures has considerable creative potential, so perhaps we should ask how to correlate it with love, especially with the love of Christ that is the great treasure Christians spontaneously seek to preserve. The creative potential in the effort to rethink the relationship between Jesus and other soteriological figures is obvious: were it to bring significant understanding, it might enhance our awareness of God's work in all parts of the world. It might also enhance our mutual appreciation, lessening the divisions we have built up to separate ourselves as Muslims and Christians, Muslims and Jews, Hindus and Muslims, Buddhists and Hindus, and on and on. And it might even lessen the tensions that precipitate violence and war, a possibility that a mere glance at the headlines about Lebanon or the West Bank of the Jordan is bound to make precious.

It is not enough, though, to place Christ in the context of other soteriological figures and cogitate about a universal theology that might give all such figures equal weight and do its work on the basis of the collectivity of their data. One has to love the prospect of seeing mutual illumination flash by comparing Christ and the Buddha, or Christ and Muhammad, or Christ and the torah. To be Christian, this exercise has to love the revelations of the divine compassion that such a resetting of Jesus occasions, noting how the depth of Jesus' prayer is spotlighted by eastern meditation, or how the sovereignty of Jesus' Father is spotlighted by Muslim faith, or how Jesus personalizes the intentions of yoga, or how Jesus tames the fear of the Lord hymned in the psalms, making it the reverence of a trusting child.

The most creative entry into religious dialogue, or into such other dialogues as that between cosmology and Christian theology or that between humanistic psychology and Christian spirituality, depends on a love of Christ that expects to find in the new conversation a challenging ratification of old iconic convictions. From the Christian side, one has to realize that nothing can separate us from the love of God in Christ Jesus, as Paul saw, and so trust that any new information, theoretical insight, or political proposal of promise can be turned to good effect. Such turning to good effect emphatically does not mean refusing to hear what one's interlocutor has to say on his or her own terms, or jumping in with apologetic arguments to defend a supposedly vulnerable Christ, or striving to convert the interlocutor to Christian faith. The prejudice (pre-judgment) on which it depends is more basic and less distorting than any such tactics. The only thing that the committed Christian brings to dialogues with non-Christians is a firm trust that honesty and good will will magnify the iconic Christ. This is the intellectual equivalent of the blank check one finally has to write God concerning one's personal struggles in the cloud of unknowing or with the paradoxes of providence.

How can one write God such an intellectual blank check in good conscience? By reconsidering the implications of a Christian commitment. What a Christian commitment boils down to is simply, and momentously, trusting that Jesus has the words of everlasting life—that Jesus ought to be one's hermeneutic (interpretational key) for the bedrock issues: death, evil, reasons to hope, reasons to love. To accept, or reject, Jesus at this level demands a leap, more or less continuous with one's assessment of the data most crucial to one's instincts about the ultimate significance of human existence. One never has an air-tight argument, for or against. True, most people shy away from Christ, and many people cling to Christ, with far less rationality and deliberation than we are implying. However, that does not invalidate our delineation of the core issue. It merely validates, in tones one hopes are more compassionate than cynical, T. S. Eliot's notion that humankind cannot bear much reality. If one tries to bear reality, to deal with the bedrock challenges and mysteries of human existence, one is bound to realize that faith is involved. There is no way to escape putting one's judgment, one's will, one's love, one's self on the line and choosing— taking a stand, making a commitment, confessing one's god or God.

At this level, having made one's confession, one is relatively impervious to new data or arguments swirling on the level of the upper, academic or organizational mind. True, ideas can have weighty personal consequences, and faith is never something settled once and for all. But the faith that has become a personal sojourning with God, no matter how dark and occasionally agitated, is not likely to be thrown onto an entirely new track, let alone into shipwreck, by an ecumenical dialogue. It is more likely to be stimulated, challenged positively—all the more so when the dialogue is personal, honest, and confessional. Meeting a sincere Muslim, Jew, Buddhist, Hindu, or even atheist, the mature Christian is more likely to find signs of the divine truth and beauty than threats to his or her Christian faith. And after the dialogue, when the Christian settles back for reflective assessment, the likelihood is that he or she will receive an invitation to take everything significant, whether attractive or troubling, to God in prayer. As the traditional teachings associated with the discernment of spirits suggest, we ought always to pay special attention to the things that have consoled or disturbed us, opening our experiences to the Holy Spirit and trying to meet the challenge or accept the greater love that they disclose. The blank check that we write to God assures that neither we nor the truth can come out losers. If the atheist shows us solid reasons for doubting the existence of God, the truth in such reasons becomes another occasion to praise "God," who of course is present in all truth, who of course can be converted with "Truth." Then we realize, once again, that God is so full a reality that God is bound to be mysterious, and that the mysteriousness of God houses all that God is not (all the critiques of bad theology and immature religion) as well as all that God is. The love of God therefore inspires the most creative interreligious dialogues, which from the Christian side are bound to seem further reasons for blessing the complete embrace of the human condition that the Logos has accomplished in Jesus.

Summary Reflections I: The Christ To Whom To Pray

What is the gist for Christian prayer of these various ruminations that the recent challenge to the uniqueness of Christ has stimulated? Considering Christ in the context of the world religions, of the rise of modern historical consciousness, of the world's need for social justice, and the like, what ought one to feel about him or say to him when one falls on one's knees? Naturally, answers to these questions can vary considerably, and no one pair of ruminators has a privileged pipeline to the Holy Spirit. Our answers, then, are simply our own, offered for whatever help they may provide others wrestling with the implications that world religions have for a Catholic Christian spirituality.

First, we think that Christians aware of the riches of meditation, social service, and profound reflection (leading to salvation) outside the borders of institutional Christianity can pray to the Word of God most gratefully. Clearly, the divine self-expression has reached to the ends of the earth, moving myriads of people to open their hearts and let their minds be drawn away from selfishness, toward transcendent wisdom. The Christian aware of the patristic traditions about the Logos of God can easily consider the riches of non-Christian spirituality the good effects of the Word in which all of creation holds together. Without distorting the self-understanding of Buddhists, Muslims, or any others who have been enriched by this Word, Christians on their knees in grateful prayer can believe that the final significance such enrichment of non-Christians holds for Christian faith is the magnification of the Logos and the further humbling of his unprofitable servants. If those unprofitable servants thought that God's grace and salvation were limited to explicitly Christian symbols, concepts, ceremonies, institutions, or ethics, they need another meditation. The obvious fact is that God has always been much greater than the Christian community, and that the Christian conviction about the necessity of the Christian community for salvation can be understood as part of the exemplary causality associated with Christ, the head of that community. In other words, one can interpret the sayings of the New Testament, the church fathers, and the later doctrinal tradition about the uniqueness of Christ and the necessity of belonging to Christ's church as pointing to the place where once and for all God disclosed the substance of the divine plan for all human beings. One does not have to require all human beings to associate themselves with Christ and the church in formal terms, though one is bound as a Christian to hope for that. The Logos assumed certain limitations in taking flesh, entering into history, and one central such limitation was agreeing to let the single, comprehensive gift of salvation be mediated through many different cultural forms. All such forms, in Christian perspective, are best understood in function of the one privileged paradigm of Jesus Christ, but faith in the real divinity of Christ, the real identification between Christ and the Logos, allows the Christian to associate all of the forms that mediate salvation with the omnipresence of the Logos and so of Christ.

In praying to the omnipresent, omnirelevant Jesus, one is not approaching a stranger. He is the same Christ one has known and approached from childhood, or from the time of one's conversion, only now one has gained a new appreciation of his grandeur. If it is appealing, one can simply admire this newly appreciated grandeur, considering it just a fuller luster adorning the sacramental Christ. Or one can speak out one's words of admiration to Christ on the cross, Jesus in the wilderness, Jesus giving himself as the bread of life—whatever one's favorite New Testament mystery. One can even let the entire further adornment of Jesus prompted by one's new appreciation of the universality of the Logos ferry one deeper into the cloud, becoming happier than ever simply to praise wordlessly and love non-conceptually the incomprehensible, present-yet-ungraspable, divine mystery.

We have noted that Christian prayer is the place where the blank check implied by deep faith comes to special prominence. The God whose face one seeks may decide to withhold it. Our own sense of guilt or unworthiness may keep us fleeing the divine silence, afraid of genuine intimacy with Christ. Or we may feel ground down by the demands of ordinary times, the great stretch of the liturgical year and the normal life-cycle when little is especially exciting, when the test is to eat and sleep and work while only seeing through a glass darkly, never seeing face to face.[5] Compared to the tests of ordinary time, the regular demand that we keep going even though we can't sense much progress, new ideas about the presence of salvation outside of institutional Christianity are bound to seem minor challenges. Certainly, we should try to give any idea, new or old, that comes to us with significant credentials an honest hearing. Certainly, we should pray about it and let it have its proper impact on our sense of the Christian mysteries. But in the measure that we are growing aware that God's regular presence is mysterious, all ideas have limited significance. If they seem disturbing, we should console ourselves with the reminder that death and evil and the crucifixion of Christ are much more disturbing. If they seem exhilarating, we should restrain ourselves with the reminder that divine life and love and the resurrection of Christ are much more exhilarating. When Saint Teresa of Avila counseled, "Let nothing disturb you," she was probably caught in the grip of the utter primacy of the divine mystery she believed, in virtue of Christ, was love. That is the sort of counsel we think most pertinent to the implications of the world religions, or of most anything else, for a Catholic Christian spirituality.

The words associated with John the Baptist, to the effect that he ought to decrease in importance and Jesus increase, fix in mind an important characteristic of Christian prayer. As it matures, it makes God much more significant and self much less significant. Among the things that a less significant self gladly sheds are anxieties that one might call self-concerns. The advice of Jesus to consider the lilies of the field, and bolster one's conviction that God will provide all the more for his human creatures, runs in this direction. We are not the best caretakers of our own selves. God is the best caretaker, so the wisest thing we can do is place ourselves in God's keeping. Interestingly, writing God a blank check, abandoning ourselves to divine providence, is also wonderfully freeing. We don't have to drag half as much ego around. We can experience what Buddhists no doubt experience when they penetrate the illusions of selfhood.

This does not mean, of course, that we are likely to attain the degree of abandonment and loss of self-concern that characterizes the saints. It does not mean that we do not continue to have worldly responsibilities. It simply means that when we pray to Christ about any of our responsibilities or worries or hopes, we can let ourselves be carried by Christ's Spirit to a simpler communication, in which we hand everything we have into Christ's keeping and ask him to be the savior our faith says he has always been.

Once and for all, Christian faith says, God gave the world a pledge of the divine love and showed the divine love to be more powerful, more beautiful, than anything that might threaten human existence. Once and for all, God expressed the divine will to save all human beings and bring them into divine life. This eschatological declaration and accomplishment of God occurred in Jesus of Nazareth, the Christ and Logos enfleshed, who was crucified and raised for all of us human beings and our salvation. Those are the words of everlasting life, and they should be enough for us. What more do we need? What more could God have given us?

Summary Reflections II: The Christ To Serve

These are rhetorical questions. There is nothing more that we need when we have appreciated God's gift of eschatological salvation in Christ. There is nothing more that God could have given us when we realize that such gracious love of God means eternal life, divinization.

What follow on these rhetorical questions, which stop the mouth and mind of the faithful Christian, are practical questions: What ought we to do about this great gift? What are the behavioral consequences of believing that in Jesus Christ God's yes to the world has sounded once and for all?

Among the countless responses that one could imagine, perhaps those most typical of the saints, the exemplary followers of Christ, boil down to imitating Christ in spending oneself to publish the good news of God's eschatological gift. Such "publication" has been by word, yes, but even more by example and ministerial (serving) deed. Having taken to heart the salvation offered them in Jesus the Christ, the Christian saints have found that they had to go and do likewise: return love for love, feed the flock committed to their keeping. The Christ they have sought to serve by spending themselves publishing the gospel has been the complete fulfillment of their hearts. By many titles—Teacher, Lord, God, Friend, Lover, and more—he has satisfied their deepest hunger and made their yoke seem easy and their burden light.

In imitation of their Lord and lover, the Christian saints have tried to promote the well-being of their brothers and sisters. Such well-being is many-sided, yet its crux is clearly union with God, without whom any worldly success would ring hollow. If people gain union with God by accepting the divine persons into their hearts and abiding with them, people are a success. Regardless of their financial status, their standing in the world of work or among the barons of society, they have found the one thing necessary. Regardless even of their brains and virtue, they have fought their way, or stumbled, or been dragged into the magic circle where all their failures are redeemed, all their dross is turned into gold.

Catholic spirituality has also sought the well-being associated with a fully healthy culture: sound bodies, sound family lives, sound minds, sound arts and sciences, sound economies, sound political arrangements. Whatever helps human beings to grow up strong and straight has to be pleasing to God. God is no enemy of human flourishing. God does not want people to be weak or ignorant. The glory of God is human beings fully alive: laughing, creating, standing by one another, braving the storms in trust that their redeemer liveth. So every parent, teacher, nurse, honest tradesman, artisan, farmer, and clerk can make a significant contribution to what God wants to happen among human beings. Every citizen of the state and member of the church has the opportunity to further the gospel's taking root and inspiring a common life worthy of the incarnate Word. That the Logos has taken flesh means that flesh could be wonderful: transparent to the beauty of God. That the anointed one of God has been willing to suffer and die for his convictions about the value of human beings means that flesh is worth far more than human beings themselves usually reckon. In the resurrection of Christ and sending of the Spirit to be the helper of those the earthly Christ has left behind, God has sealed this series of judgments. During the interval between Christ's resurrection and his return to consummate history, his people have only to abide in his love and they will prosper and bear much fruit.

Living from such abiding, such contemplative immersion in the love of the divine persons, the followers of Christ are bound to be good servants of their Lord and his gospel. They are bound to give good example at work. They are not bound, but they are inclined, to reflect on the problems they meet in the light of their abiding with God and find challenging hypotheses about how to solve them. Why couldn't people alleviate the problem of poverty by sharing their possessions more generously? Why should age or sex or race or religion have to be a source of discrimination and division? How important, after all, are money, status, worldly power, prestige? They did not matter much to Christ, and they get little attention in the peak moments when our abiding with God is palpable. But if they are not very important, why couldn't people feel free to work mainly to make beautiful things that would please the human spirit, or to make useful things that would ease others' burdens, or to help nature stay healthy and bountiful, or to guide the next generation on the straight path?

The Christ the saints have sought to serve is a bringer of freedom as well as of salvation. The second name of his salvation is liberation. Contemplating him, abiding with his Father and Spirit, one senses how few things are compulsory, how many good deeds flow connaturally, when one is in love with the Love that moves the stars. Basking in the flow of the sacramental Christ, people grow confident that they know what human flesh, human time, human talent are for. They are to adorn the world and sing the praises of the world's creator. They are to echo the refrain of Genesis that God knows that the things he has made are very good.

All the more painful, therefore, have been the saints' encounters with evil, both that of other people and that lurking in their own breasts. Like Christ, the saints soon learn to consider sin a powerful reality, but they never learn to accept it as ordinary or natural. Constantly, it remains the mystery of iniquity, a mind-boggling surd. Jesus hanging from the cross summarizes the depths of this iniquity, but even Jesus cannot make it intelligible. The only sense it has is lost in God, who has contrived to make grace abound over sin and use the cross of Christ to mediate everlasting life. Standing before such sense, the saints can only bow low and feel hymns of praise redoubling in their hearts.

How does one serve to others the sobering news of the depravity disclosed in human sin? Only by coupling it with the transporting news that God has used sin to bring about a much more impressive order of grace. By itself the cross of Christ is not only incomplete, it is distorting. As the blazing christology of Paul makes plain, the cross of Christ is related dialectically to his victory, his rising to the right hand of the Father. The obedience that Christ showed his Father, which is a paradigm for all Christians, became the cause of his exaltation. In taking Christ to himself, the Father promised to take all who centered in Christ as well. Christ was the first of many brothers and sisters. In preaching about him, those serving his cause can promise those who embrace him an exaltation like his own.

But haven't the saints suffered greatly for their allegiance to Christ, their service of a good news calling the world to repent? Haven't they been carried into the mystery of Christ's sufferings, so that they have lost their lives in order to gain them? Yes indeed. Despite such sufferings, however, they have tended to follow Paul in counting their losses gains. If they lived, they had Christ, and if they died, they could hope to have Christ more fully. The world, for all its beauty and winsome need, was passing. Only Christ was the same yesterday, today, and tomorrow. The poor were always with them, seeking a cup of cold water in Christ's name but not exhausting the fullness of what God's kingdom implied. When Christ handed over that kingdom to his Father, and the Father was all in all, the poor would be no more. All 144,000 of the saints would be completely rich.

Hoping for God's triumph in every person's heart, for the loss of none whom the Father has put into Christ's keeping, the missionary saints have set out for the farthest corners of the globe, confident that the love God has revealed in Christ is exactly what all people need. In our opinion, Catholic Christians entering upon interreligious dialogue today do best when they draw upon such confidence of their saintly predecessors and make it the basis of their own service of the iconic Christ.

NOTES

1. See Eric Voegelin, ORDER AND HISTORY, 5 vols. (Baton Rouge: Louisiana State University Press, 1956–87), especially volume 4. See also our INTERPRETING THE RELIGIOUS EXPERIENCE (Englewood Cliffs, N.J.: Prentice-Hall, 1987), which applies Voegelin to the world religions. For a Lonerganian approach to the relationship between spirituality and the world religions, see Vernon Gregson, LONERGAN, SPIRITUALITY, AND THE MEETING OF RELIGIONS (Lanham, MD: University Press of America, 1985).

2. See Edward Stevens, SPIRITUAL TECHNOLOGIES (New York: Paulist Press, 1989). How Christian this book is is questionable, but it owes much to such Christian attempts to appropriate techniques of eastern spirituality as Anthony de Mello's SADHANA: A WAY TO GOD (St. Louis: Institute of Jesuit Sources, 1978) and Hugo Enomiya-Lassalle's LIVING IN THE NEW CONSCIOUSNESS (Boston: Shambhala Publications, 1988).

3. See, for example, Richard Ford, THE SPORTSWRITER (New York: Vintage, 1986); Raymond Carver, WHERE I'M CALLING FROM (New York: Vintage, 1989); David Leavett, EQUAL AFFECTIONS (New York: Weidenfeld & Nicholson, 1989). Of the three, Leavett seems the most aware of the positive possibilities in religious faith.

4. On the value of the experience of the saints for theology, see William M. Thompson, FIRE AND LIGHT: THE SAINTS AND THEOLOGY (New York: Paulist, 1986).

5. For a lovely approach to prayer as a personal relationship based on scripture, see William A. Barry, S. J., SEEK MY FACE (New York: Paulist, 1989). For a powerful novel describing the daily struggle for faith and meaning, see A. G. Mojtabai, ORDINARY TIME (New York: Doubleday, 1989).

Index

other books from the Carmodys
published by Paulist Press

BONDED IN CHRIST'S LOVE
PEACE AND JUSTICE IN THE SCRIPTURES
  OF THE WORLD RELIGIONS
WHAT ARE THEY SAYING ABOUT NON-CHRISTIAN FAITH?